D1109238

EARL
WARREN

BOOKS BY IRVING STONE

BIOGRAPHICAL NOVELS

IMMORTAL WIFE
(Jessie Benton Fremont)

LUST FOR LIFE
(Vincent Van Gogh)

SAILOR ON HORSEBACK
(Jack London)

ADVERSARY IN THE HOUSE
(Eugene V. Debs)

BIOGRAPHIES

EARL WARREN

CLARENCE DARROW FOR THE DEFENSE

THEY ALSO RAN

FICTION

FALSE WITNESS

PAGEANT OF YOUTH

BELLES-LETTRES

DEAR THEO
(The Autobiography of Vincent Van Gogh)

EARL WARREN

A Great American Story

by

Irving Stone

Prentice-Hall, Inc.
New York

FOR JEAN

(who reorganizes)

I wish to acknowledge my indebtedness to the editors of *Life* magazine for permission to use material from my article, "The Case for Warren," published in their May 10, 1948, issue; and to the *Town Meeting of the Air* for permission to use material from my broadcast of June 8, 1948, "Whom Should the Republicans Nominate?"

—IRVING STONE

Contents

EARL
WARREN

I. Prologue

OUTSIDE the California Senate is a wooden railing with a sign which reads TAKE NOTICE: NO LOBBYING IN SENATE CHAMBER. No such railing is needed in front of the Governor's permanently open door: few paid lobbyists have been rash enough to venture into Earl Warren's office in the six years of his governorship.

During the thirteen years that he was district attorney of Alameda County, no case that Warren tried was reversed by a higher court, nor was any complaint ever lodged against his methods by the ever-vigilant American Civil Liberties Union. He prosecuted only when he had to, and when his evidence was complete. "I never heard a jury bring in a verdict of guilty," says Warren, "but that I felt sick at the pit of my stomach."

He is without rancor, tension or bitterness; even his political adversaries like and respect him. Democratic Governor Culbert Olson, whom Warren defeated in the heated campaign of 1942, says of him today, "Earl Warren has grown amazingly with the passage of the years." Robert W. Kenny, who was the Democratic

1

attorney general during Warren's first term, and whom Warren defeated for the governorship in 1946, says, "He is delightful to work with, and his appointments are ninety-eight percent excellent." Warren's good friend, Harold Stassen, says, "Earl Warren comes up on the right side of all human issues."

His personality and methods of work are bland; when he loses an issue he remains friends with the men who defeated him, though they know that he is a persistent fighter who will be back again next week or next year with the bill he feels is needed. When he took over the governorship, California was churned by feuds and social and political war. Warren has had a salutary effect on the state, binding its wounds, removing many sources of infection.

His outstanding characteristic is a distrust of power; he believes in government by law, and not by executive decree. He repudiates the concept of The Leader or The Superman as injurious to the well-being of a democracy. When he was re-elected by both parties in 1946, with the strongest mandate ever vouchsafed to a California governor, he might have considered himself justified in a seizure of all the power he could grab; yet he wanted, and took, no whit more of control than he had exercised during his first term. His satisfactions come from being of service; he has no omnivorous ego to feed.

He is the first since Hiram Johnson, in 1915, to be re-elected governor, and only the third to be re-elected in the century of the state's history. Yet he has no personal machine, and makes no effort to control the Republican structure. "No man can do his job as governor," says Warren, "and run a political machine at the same time."

Perhaps for this reason he has the most completely nonpartisan record on the American scene. When he ran for attorney general in 1938, he filed on the Republican, Democratic and Progressive tickets; this cross-filing is legal in the state, and a practice followed by most candidates. Warren received the nomination from all three parties, and that was the end of the election! In 1946 he again was nominated by both parties in the primary, with almost as many Democrats voting for him as did Republicans. His nature is not partisan, prejudiced, one-sided; he can perceive many shades between black and white and he fears above all the closed minds of the extreme right and extreme left.

Earl Warren is a tall, broad-shouldered, open-faced man with a warm personality and a passionate dedication to logical and humane government. He likes people, and people find it as easy and natural to like him as they do to breathe. They seem to vote for him with the same facility.

Recently Governor Warren sent his annual budget to the legislature, asking for a near-billion dollars for state expenditures (by far the largest appropriation in the Union); and it was asked of a traditionally conservative legislature. The assembled legislators hardly blinked as Governor Warren read his message, asking for hundreds of millions for education, for public health, for child centers and hospitals, for roads, colleges, in what is probably the most vigorously progressive program in America today, and one of the most far-seeing in terms of the growth of the state and the future well-being of its citizens. The legislature passed Governor Warren's budget because they knew that it was scientifically constructed, without a dollar for the pork barrel.

What manner of young Lochinvar is this, come out of the West? What are the roots of his vision, and his courage? What goes into the making of a modern, freedom-loving and conscientious American?

II. From These Beginnings

EARL WARREN is the son of Methias H. Warren, who was born in Stavanger, Norway, and who was brought to the United States as an infant. The family settled at Eagle Grove, Iowa. Methias' mother died when he was four and when he was seven he went to live with a neighboring farm family, where he helped with the chores in return for his keep. During the winter he went to the neighborhood school, managing to get as far as the seventh grade. To the end of his days there burned in Methias Warren a hunger for knowledge, for training, for education; perhaps the greatest of his life's ambitions was to send his children to the university. He had never seen the outside of a college, nor had known what went on inside, yet his instincts told him that through education would come independence and the good full life.

Methias' father remarried, and neither the young boy nor his older brother was comfortable at home. They began to wander over the Midwest, working the harvests of Iowa and Minnesota in the summer, finding occasional jobs as mechanics during the winter months. Neither of the Warren boys was very strong; when Methias was nineteen and his brother twenty-one, they found themselves in Chicago, in the bitterest weather, and broke. The brother came down with tuberculosis. Methias nursed him as best he could in a cold, barren room. They had no money for a doctor or hospital or medicines. The boy died in Methias' arms.

This was the most searing experience in young Methias' life, one he was never to forget and one which would shape irrevocably his character: for Methias Warren remained convinced that his brother's life could have been saved if they had had money for a doctor and a hospital. To Earl he said over and over again: "Son, never let yourself be caught broke."

Methias returned to Minnesota. After a few months of unhappiness and aloneness he met a girl by the name of Crystal Hernlund who had been born in Helsingland, Sweden, and who also had been brought to this country as a baby. The Hernlund family had settled in Chicago, but when they lost their home in the great fire of 1871 the family moved to Minneapolis, where Methias and Crystal fell in love and married. A daughter, whom they named Ethel, was born the following year.

Methias' health had not improved with the years; remembering the fate of his brother he decided to take his family out to the warm dry climate of California. They settled first in San Diego, but Methias could not find the kind of skilled employment that he wanted. Their next move was one hundred and twenty miles up the coast to Los Angeles, where he found a job with the Southern Pacific Railroad as a car repairer, the kind of mechanical work he liked, and in which he saw a good future. They rented a small frame house at 458 Turner Street down near the wooden railroad station, and here Earl was born on March 19, 1891. Years later when Earl asked, "Father, why didn't you give me a middle initial?" Methias replied with a laugh:

"Son, when you were born we were too poor to enjoy any luxury of that kind."

The Warrens were a happy family, not overly demonstrative, but intensely loyal to each other. Methias was a good-looking man with wide, gray eyes and a full mustache curled just slightly at the edges. Earl's mother, whom he resembled, had large blue eyes, a fair, pink complexion, a full sensitive mouth and wore her dark brown hair tied tight back with forehead bangs. In a picture taken in 1894, Methias stands proudly behind his wife and two children, with a high starched collar, and a white tie, a starched bosom shirt and a black cutaway coat, his hair parted gently on the left side, mighty proud of his handsome wife in her puff-sleeved taffeta, of Ethel in her velvet guimpe, and of blond, blue-eyed, tow-haired Earl with a lace-edged Lord Fauntleroy collar tucked under his chin. It is the picture of a contented and prosperous family.

Crystal Warren was a quiet, simple woman, completely devoted to her family and her home, not saying very much even in moments of trouble or crisis. She kept her two children scrubbed and healthy; since she too was ambitious to see them rise in the world, she made endless personal sacrifices so that the family could

save part of Methias' seventy-dollar-a-month wage.
Earl was deeply attached to his mother.

By the time Earl was four, the Warrens had rented a
bungalow just across the street from the Ann Street
School. It was in connection with this school that Earl
had his only two memories of Los Angeles, the one
pleasant, when his sister sometimes took him to class
with her; the other frightening and brutal, searing itself upon his mind as deeply as had the death of his uncle
seared itself upon Methias' mind.

The year before, Eugene V. Debs had formulated the
first industrial union known in America, called the
American Railway Union. It embraced members from
the highest of the skilled crafts down to the lowliest
trackwalker and seamstress in the Pullman factory.
Methias and his comrades in the Southern Pacific shops
had promptly joined this union, and when Debs called
a strike in 1894, Methias put down his tools and walked
out of the railroad yards. It is difficult for a working man with young children to leave his job for an in-
determinate period, and lose his wages. For Methias this
was more than difficult, it was almost an heroic accomplishment; Earl's father had never forgotten that he had
lost his brother because they had had no money, and was
congenitally incapable of spending a dollar on himself.
Mrs. Warren and the two children had everything they
needed, but the house was run under an austere economy. Methias' loyalty to his comrades proved stronger
than his phobia about money and savings. One day Earl
stood in the yard of the Ann Street School and watched
the strikers hoist a straw figure on the school's flagpole,
thus hanging in effigy one of the railroad managers.

Today, some fifty-three years later, Earl Warren becomes pale and tense when he relives the scene, for this act of mock violence became a symbol in the boy's mind of the futility of intemperate thinking and quarrelsome conduct between peoples who are differing, whether it be over wages, policy, opinion or ideas.

Methias Warren and the railroaders remained out on strike for several months, while the family's savings were eaten up. To make matters worse, Debs and his fellow officers were thrown into jail, the strike broken, and the A.R.U. permanently smashed. Methias and his comrades not only were fired by the Southern Pacific, but blacklisted. The members of the A.R.U. lost their homes, savings, security, many of them wandering the roads for years like tramps, unable to find employment.

Methias too had to leave his family and go out into the Mojave desert region to secure work from the Santa Fe. To young Earl Warren this vengeful act on the part of the railroads seemed the same kind of violence as that of the strikers hanging a manager in effigy. Thus he saw the reverse side of the shield, and this use of force became equally distasteful and frightening to him. In this sense the major portion of the young boy's character was already formed by the time he left Los Angeles at the age of four.

After several months Methias learned that the Southern Pacific was moving its railroad yards from Tulare to Bakersfield. He reasoned that the railroad's need for skilled workmen would be so great that the company might be willing to let bygones be bygones. He went to

Bakersfield at once, secured employment as a car repairer and very quickly brought his family to the hot
little valley town of Kern City, a railroad cluster just a
mile away from Bakersfield, which had been settled by
railroad men and was the headquarters for the French
and Basque sheepherders who kept their flocks in the
surrounding hills. Methias rented a bungalow on Sum-
ner Street just across from the railroad yards.

The local school which Earl entered when he was six
was tough and riotous. Some of the fifteen- and
sixteen-year-old grammar students were practically
grown men. Earl remembers these roughnecks standing
out in the school yard, threatening the unpopular principal to come out and have his block knocked off.
There was a great deal of insubordination and truancy,
with rulers swishing down across the students' hands
and straps across their posteriors. The first principal
resigned; the succeeding principal, Leo Pauley, was a
big kindly man who could handle the tough youngsters.
Earl was never a fractious student, but occasionally he
got out of line and for these transitory pleasures he still
has a vivid image of the descending ruler and strap.
There was no supervision of recreation or athletics; the
boys spent their recesses and play hours in fist-fighting.
Earl was not only undersized for his age, but he had a
friendly, amiable nature and hated all conflict. Despite
this fact he was constantly egged on to fight by having
a whittled chip placed on his shoulder, which another
boy was badgered into knocking off, or by being jostled
against another boy on whose shoulder a chip had been
placed. In the jungle of the school yard it was a case of
the devil take the hindmost, and so Earl had to learn to

defend himself. These fights were double trouble, for his parents disapproved, and if perchance he won the first round in the school yard he was very likely to lose the second round at home, to his father.

Meanwhile Methias was working hard, and prospering. He sent away to the International Correspondence School for home courses; Earl can still see his father sitting at a little desk in front of the blazing coal stove in the dining room, working on his textbooks in mechanics and engineering. In the yards Methias had advanced to the position of master car repairer, and with his savings he built a modest house on Monterey Street. After the Warrens had developed a nice lawn and garden, they had an advantageous offer to sell; Methias promptly built another and slightly larger house. The money from the sale of this second house enabled Methias to build three new homes. The Warrens moved into one of them and rented the others to railroad families. When the second house Methias had built burned down, the Warrens got the lot back. Methias now built a comfortable home in which Earl's parents lived until the tragic murder of his father in 1938. Methias worked on the houses himself, with Earl as an assistant.

"I used to help my father with the plumbing and electrical work," says Warren, "but I might just as well have been asleep for all the good I was to him."

However, if he couldn't be a skilled mechanic, there were a lot of other jobs Earl could and did do. When he was ten years old he worked all summer on an ice wagon for twenty-five cents a day, with a chunk of ice for the family thrown in as a bonus. When he was eleven he took over two paper routes, getting up at six-thirty in the morning to distribute the Los Angeles *Herald*, then meeting the morning train at Kern City to sell papers at the station. In the afternoon he had a route for the Bakersfield *Californian*.

Methias Warren did not need his son's money, and in fact never took one penny of it, insisting that each dollar of savings be put in the bank. Methias believed that a young boy should work, and earn money, not only for the value of the savings themselves but for the discipline, and for the knowledge of how much sweat and diligence has to go into the making of any piece of change.

"Never a dollar I made was turned over to the family; my father was always glad to see me working after school, even if it was only odd jobs like distributing handbills for theaters and circuses. But when I brought the change home he would say, 'Put it away, son, you will need it. Never let yourself get caught broke.'"

During the following two summers Earl drove grocery wagons drawn by mules, and one year he drove a delivery wagon every day after school. He also sold books and leather-bound sets, such as *The Life of McKinley*, from door to door. "I wasn't very good as a book salesman. I was shy, and couldn't talk to people." Methias had bought him the *Century Encyclopedia*, and would let him buy any book he wanted to read; but when the father failed to fall for his own son's sales talk on *The Life of McKinley*, Earl decided that he was in the wrong calling.

By the time he entered Bakersfield High School in 1904 the oil boom was on, and Bakersfield was a wide-open town in the wild and woolly tradition of the West, with as little law and order as any place in the United States. The cowboys came in on weekends dressed in their boots and spurs and flamboyant shirts and rode their horses into the saloons. The gambling houses ran twenty-four hours a day. In addition to the unruly cowboys, sheepherders and the drinking, brawling oil-men, Bakersfield, which had become an important rail-road center, was filled with "boomers," adventuresome railroad men who stayed about six months in each new and exciting town, then boomed along. There were large red-light districts, and lots of gun play, with men being shot for jumping oil claims; the law-enforcement officers were practically powerless. Warren recalls the shooting fracas in which Lawrence Tibbett's father, who was sheriff of the county, and Tibbett's uncle, who was Chief of Police of Bakersfield, were both shot to death: An escaped prisoner by the name of McKinney had been terrorizing the neighborhood by forcing his way into farmhouses, ordering the man of the house to shave him, and then shooting the farmer by way of compensation.

McKinney and a henchman by the name of Al Hultse were trailed to a Chinese joss house, where, in the course of the next few hours, the Tibbett brothers were shot to death by Hultse; when McKinney finally stuck his head out of the door he had it blown off.

Hearing of this excitement, Earl rode over to the scene on Jack, his burro. When told about the incredibly accurate shooting which had come from the joss house, there flashed into his mind a turkey shoot he had attended. One participant had collected a turkey for practically every shot, and while sorting them, he had tossed a wild white turkey to Earl, saying, "Here, son, take this one home with you." Standing before the joss house, Earl somehow knew that the man who had been shooting so accurately from within, and the person who gave him the turkey, must be one and the same. Later, when he went into the courtroom to hear Al Hultse's trial and got his first look at the man since the shooting, he saw that he had been right in his assumption.

Earl's parents were considerably disturbed about their son growing up in such a wild town, where there was every opportunity for misadventure, and where the doors of the saloons and gambling joints were open even to children. Methias had never taken a drink in his life, and never kept liquor in his house. Neither had he gambled.

"Father never was one to preach," says Warren; "he did not try to restrict my activities." Earl would occasionally wander into a gambling joint where he was fascinated by the stacks of gold piled up on the tables. He tried his luck once or twice, but during the dull hours, when there was no one else around, the dealers and croupiers showed the boy how they dealt from the bottom of the deck, and sneaked loaded dice into the crap game.

"They showed off their skill with all the pride of the professional," says Warren; and later when he found himself surrounded by crooked gamblers in Alameda County he recalled these early lessons in the art and fraud of gambling.

He grew up a normal, active, likable boy. His parents encouraged him to keep chickens, rabbits and dogs in the back yard and to raise vegetables and take care of the fruit trees. The burro they had bought him became his chief companion, and carried him over the mountains on numerous pack and camping trips. Despite this vigorous outdoor life, he was growing slowly.

"Another boy and I were the only ones who had to go through our freshman year at Bakersfield High School in knee pants. Believe me, that was a sore trial! Most of the boys were above average in age and size, and I was below, so they kind of coddled me."

Earl rode his bicycle to and from school, and since the route went through the County Court yard he frequently stopped off to listen to the criminal cases. However, his desire to become a lawyer antedates these exciting trials.

"My determination to become a lawyer goes back so far that I can hardly remember ever having been without it."

In high school he was most interested in history, devouring the *Leather-Stocking Tales,* and the novels of G. A. Henty. In his senior year the history teacher said to him, "The only reason I don't give you a hundred is that I have scruples against giving anybody a hundred." His second keenest interest was in the English classes, but as his father had suspected, he had no talent whatever for the sciences. He did so poorly in physics that he later had to take the entrance examination in order to get into the University of California.

When he was fourteen, Earl decided that he wanted to work in the railroad yards. Methias was now foreman of the repair shops, and it was a simple matter for him to have the boy taken on. However, before he would let him start with the railroads, he extracted two promises from his son:

"Earl, you must give me your word of honor that you will put your earnings in a bank account. And when the summer is over, you will go back to school."

When he was fifteen, he worked the entire summer as a call boy on the railroad. His twelve-hour day was spent going to the saloons and every place else he could think of to round up the train crews when they were due in for their runs. He was paid twenty-two cents an hour, and had to put in a seven-day week. The following summer he got a job in the machine shop as a steamfitter's and machinist's helper. Here his wage was raised to twenty-five cents an hour for a ten-hour day, but once again he confesses:

"I had no talent or interest in machinery, and as a helper I wasn't much help. I was exposed to first-rate mechanics for years, and yet I carried away no mechanical knowledge from all that experience."

Earl's parents believed that every child should have a musical education. They had bought his sister a piano on which she was taking lessons, and in the parlor there was also a standing Victrola with a large music cabinet. Methias now bought Earl a clarinet, and the boy took two lessons a week from a private teacher. He quickly found a place in the town band, and then became a charter member of the Musicians Union in Bakersfield.

"I always had a devil of a lot to do," says Warren, "I played for town dances, was on the high-school baseball team in my senior year, and worked every spare hour in the railroad shops. I wasn't much interested in girls;

there was an occasional dance at the high school, but I rarely went."

At the age of seventeen he was ready to enter the University of California at Berkeley. He had eight hundred dollars which he had saved up from his odd jobs, but this was his money to spend as he wished, for Methias Warren gave him an ample allowance. As Earl went out the front door of the bungalow, Methias said:

"Well, my boy, you are going away from home. You are a man now, and I am sure you are going to act like one."

His admonition was considerably premature. Though Earl had sprouted up to five feet eleven, he was as skinny as the Southern Pacific rails that ran through Kern City. He had played baseball for Bakersfield High, but he was not athletic by nature, preferring the less competitive sports of swimming, fishing, hunting jack rabbits with a slingshot, and going on camping trips. He still probably preferred the company of Jack, his burro, to the prettiest girl in the county. His childhood had been vigorous, and completely undistinguished. He wanted to become a trial lawyer, but actually had little concept of what this might mean. He was practical of mind but not particularly ambitious, easygoing, open and likable, and still adolescent in a lean, lanky, and friendly fashion.

III. Youth Is an Interesting Time

"WHEN I got up to Berkeley," says Warren, "it was just like being in a wonderland; it was the new life, the new freedom, the companionship, the romance of the University, the newborn loyalties. I am afraid I didn't have any craving for knowledge, and I never thought of the University as representing the one great opportunity of my life. I was young, immature, very much the Freshman, and I was known by that name. No book or professor had a profound influence on me, not even in the law school. Companionship was the greatest thing I found at the University, and it still stands out in my mind today as more important than anything I learned in classes."

He lived at the La Junta Club on College Avenue. With no work to do except a very modest amount of studying, and with the opportunity to consume endless hot dogs and coffee from Bill the Dog Man, he put on thirty pounds during his first semester, partially filling out his skinny frame. The La Junta Club received a charter from the Sigma Phi Fraternity, and

Warren lived here during his six years at the University.

He met regularly with a convivial group of boys at Pop Kessler's restaurant, where they ate their steaks smothered in onions, washed down with innumerable mugs of beer, then sang college songs, barbershop ballads, and recited sentimental poetry from slim volumes which they carried in their hip pockets. One of Warren's classmates stoutly maintains that Earl was an elegant declaimer of such immortal bits as *The Sinking of the Mary Gloucester*. He particularly enjoyed reading the humorous verse of the San Francisco poet, Gelett Burgess, a former University of California student, who was now the patron saint of the club.

Before college Earl never before had slept away from his parents. Though his home life had been completely happy, it had been a trifle on the austere side. These gay years were a valuable interlude.

As a prelegal student he majored in political science, in which he earned top grades, and did quite well in history and English. He set no worlds afire in his other subjects, and there is still a canard abroad that he flunked in Greek. His friends called him by the affectionate nickname of Pinky, probably because of his light coloring and pink cheeks; but there is also the rumor that he got the name from a pretty nurse during a pink-eye epidemic on the campus. "Come on, Pinky," she said to him in front of friends who were visiting him at the infirmary, "it's time for your medicine." He wanted to be a southpaw pitcher, but he had considerable trouble finding the home plate; despite his parents' fears at his being raised in a boisterous border town, this is the only wildness of which he was guilty. As compensation for not making the varsity, he became first clarinetist in the University band. On weekends he took long walks in the beautiful Berkeley hills, which overlooked San Francisco Bay and the Golden Gate Strait. Then, suddenly, he would become homesick, and Methias would have to send him a railroad pass so that he could come down for a day or two.

During the summers he worked in the car repair shops alongside his father, who had become master car repairman for the entire division. Methias had by now built a number of cottages which he rented to the rail-roaders, and the family had a substantial income. Even so, Warren felt that he should work during the vacations, since he lived such a wonderfully carefree existence at college.

At the end of his third year, when he was twenty, he entered the first freshman class of the newly opened Boalt Hall of Law. There was nothing in his background or his three years as an undergraduate to indicate the presence of a fighter, let alone a rebel; nothing to presage his revolt against the teaching methods and cloistered attitudes, a revolt which sent him on his first important step toward maturity. However, like all of his subsequent revolts, this first one was carried on quietly, inside his head, until he had figured out a solution and a *modus operandi*.

Right from the beginning the methods and techniques of the Boalt Hall faculty irritated him.

"The law school made a fetish of discouraging the acquisition of practical knowledge; and they were so committed to the case system that they denied you the opportunity of seeing things in perspective. They started off on antique language from old English law, and didn't want anybody to read on the outside. I didn't approve of their methods of teaching and didn't like them; I said nothing, either to my fellow students or the professors, but I suppose my attitude must have been apparent. At the end of the first year when I received my A.B., but still had two years to go to secure my doctor of jurisprudence, the Dean came to me and said:

" 'Warren, I don't like to have to tell you this, but I think you should be prepared for the fact that you will never graduate.' "

Stunned, Warren could only ask, "Why? Haven't I passed my examinations?"

"Yes, you passed the written examinations," replied the Dean, "but you have never once all year volunteered to speak in class."

"Is it obligatory that one volunteer to speak in class, Dean?"

"No, it's not exactly obligatory."

"Was I ever informed that I would have to volunteer in class in order to graduate?"

"No, we simply assumed that you knew."

"Well then, Dean, as I was never told, and it is not obligatory, and I am passing my examinations, I am going to graduate."

The Dean smiled wanly. "You know of course that if you fail any one of your five remaining subjects, you won't graduate?"

Warren returned the wan smile. "Dean, I haven't

the slightest intention of flunking any one of the five remaining subjects."

The following year he took a course in constitutional law from the Dean; not once did the head of the faculty call on him to recite in class, though he called on the others frequently; and never once did Warren volunteer. The Dean was fair about the feud, giving Warren a good grade on his written examinations. Other professors called on him to recite; and sometimes, though still shy, he persuaded himself to volunteer.

The Dean's warning not only did not frighten him, but turned him even more against the rigid casebook methods. He now took the first important gamble of his life, and one that gave him shorter odds than the packed deck or loaded dice of the Bakersfield gamblers. His practical nature craved training in the everyday application of the law, and so he found a job as a clerk in a Berkeley law office where he worked in the afternoons. He had to apply himself rigorously to the books and burn the midnight oil, for a failure in any one subject, or any intimation that he was flouting the authorities of the University law school, and the Dean would unceremoniously refuse to pass him. Earl knew that such a failure would break Methias' heart; that it also would set him adrift in the world without a job, a profession, or a way of life that could interest and excite him.

He came through all right, passed all the courses, and graduated in the middle of his class. He had not been a sufficiently brilliant student to make the new *Law Review*, and no one voted for him as the Lawyer Most Likely to Succeed.

After being admitted to the Bar, he found a job in the law offices of the Associated Oil Company in San Francisco. He stayed there for one year, and then moved to Oakland to become a law clerk in the firm of Robinson and Robinson. Neither the Associated Oil Company nor Robinson and Robinson gave him any important work to do. He describes these two years as the most rugged of his life, but probably the words dreary and unpromising would be more applicable.

Though he was now twenty-three, he was a light blond with almost no beard. "I guess I must have looked awfully young to people," comments Warren wryly, ". . . for that matter, maybe I was."

He still wanted to become a trial lawyer. His hunger for the practical application of the law had grown even more acute, but he never had had an opportunity to write an opinion, go into court, or effect a compromise between disputing litigants. His wage had amounted to little more than carfare; under the circumstances that may have been all he was worth. He felt that he was wasting his time, and that the farther he trudged along this particular road, the farther away he would get from his ultimate objective.

Earl Warren was never a man of quick and easy emotion: he came to decisions slowly and painfully, rarely seeking counsel on the outside. He knew now that he had to be his own man, that he did not want to work for any more legal employers, and so he began formulating plans with two of his fellow graduates from Boalt Hall to open a law office of their own. He had no clients, and neither enough nor the right kind of experience to begin a major practice. But what alternative did he have?

Then the United States declared war on Germany, and the meager need for young lawyers in the country was suddenly supplanted by a crying need for young soldiers.

IV. "You're in the Army Now"

As soon as the first Officers Training Corps opened its doors in San Francisco, Earl Warren crossed the Bay and applied for admission. He was one of thousands, with the Army prepared to take only a few hundred; he was rejected. Hearing that there would be another group accepted within a month or two, he set out to put himself in great physical condition. This time he did better: he was accepted by the Army officers, only to be told by the examining doctor that he had hemorrhoids. Swallowing his disappointment, Warren said in effect, "Don't go away, I'll be right back."

He dashed over to Oakland, and by mid-afternoon was in the hospital, being operated on. He was confident that he would get up the next morning, return to San Francisco and be inducted into the Officers Training Corps. Instead he awakened with ether pneumonia, and was confined to his bed for three weeks. By the time he did get out of the hospital the O.T.C. had been closed, and the draft had been put into effect. Warren's number was fairly well down on the list, but he waived his immunity, and in August of 1917 was put in charge of the initial ten percent of the draftees from Oakland, and ordered to take his group to Camp Lewis near Tacoma, Washington. It was the first time Earl Warren had been given the responsibility of leadership; he managed to handle it philosophically.

At Camp Lewis he was assigned to I Company, 363rd Infantry, 91st Division, and put through basic training. At the end of four weeks he was made a first sergeant, with two hundred and fifty men under him, and supervision of the company's mess hall, barracks, clothing and equipment, office work. Thus, in addition to the regular field and drill duties of a first sergeant, he had a big organizational job to do. It was to prove his most valuable training in the Army.

On January 5, 1918, after five months of service, he was given the opportunity he had missed twice before: he was admitted to officers training at Camp Lewis. On May 1, when his course was completed, he was sent back to his original I Company for three weeks, and then on to Camp Lee, Virginia, as a replacement officer for overseas duty. Here he was commissioned a second lieutenant. Along with his comrades he confidently expected to be on his way to Europe within a matter of days. However Camp Lee became a training center, and Lieutenant Warren was kept busy with the steady influx of raw recruits. There was one commissioned officer for every squad, adding up to thirty-three second lieutenants for the company. Warren worked his way up to second in command. After a few weeks he was assigned to the bayonet school, the last form of specialization which peaceable young Warren would have chosen for himself.

"They ran us until we dropped from exhaustion; one other fellow and I were the only ones of the entire school who weren't hospitalized."

This time he figured that as soon as his bayonet training was completed he would be sent overseas; instead he was dispatched to Camp MacArthur in Waco, Texas, to teach at the central infantry officers training camp. His promotion to the rank of first lieutenant did little to solace him. He had been at Camp MacArthur only a few days when the Armistice was signed. It took a whole month, until December 11, 1918, for him to be mustered out.

Warren says, "The Army was damned hard work; there were always extra duties and extra training. I don't believe I got out of Camp Lewis more than twice, and Camp Lee more than three or four times."

He went home to Bakersfield to celebrate Christmas with his family. Since he had gained twenty-five pounds of hard flesh during his year and a half in the service, grown to his full height of six feet, one inch, and weighed an even two hundred pounds, he had told his sister to give away all his clothes. Now, at twenty-seven, his only suit was the uniform on his back, and his complete capital the sixty dollars discharge pay in his pocket. He needed a few weeks to think and take stock of himself; up to this point he had not been exactly a howling success, and his lifetime faith in the law as a way of life had thus far proved a mirage. He didn't know what he was going to do next, for his

Boalt Hall friends had been scattered by the war, and it was improbable that they could be brought together again. He did not reveal his uncertainties to his parents, nor did he tell them that his discharge pay, most of which he spent for the family Christmas presents, was the last of his cash. If he had not been a man when his father called him one at the immature age of seventeen, he was certainly a man now.

Immediately after the turn of the year, Earl went back to Oakland where he moved in with his sister Ethel, who had married Vernon Plank, a storekeeper for the Southern Pacific. After a good night's sleep and a hearty breakfast he walked downtown to the business district of Oakland. Here Fate stepped into the breach. The years of uncertainty were ended. He bumped into Leon Gray, with whom he had worked in the office of Robinson and Robinson. Gray asked what he was planning to do. Warren replied that he did not yet know. Gray said:

"I've just been elected to the state legislature to represent an Oakland district. Each legislator is entitled to place one man at five dollars a day to help with the work of the session. Why not come to Sacramento with me, and think about your future up there?"

To Warren this sounded like a very good idea. In Sacramento they met another young assemblyman, Charles Kasch, a fraternity brother of Warren's, who was also from Boalt Hall. Kasch said:

"I don't have anybody to put in a job, so let's combine and get Earl a good one."

The good one turned out to be Clerk of the Judiciary Committee, at seven dollars a day. If this was manna from heaven for Earl Warren, it was also a good deal for the judiciary committee which could not often hire doctors of jurisprudence at seven dollars a day.

Earl shared quarters with Leon Gray at the old, modest Hotel Sequoia on K Street, which was headquarters for the Alameda County legislators, local officials and attorneys who came up to the capital to transact business. Here he became acquainted with most of the important men from his home port. He was the first discharged veteran to reach Sacramento, and being tall, husky and broad-shouldered, he looked very fetching in his officer's uniform. The legislators took a liking to him. One of his closest friendships was formed with thirty-year-old Frank Anderson, a frail, dark-complexioned legislator who had been a representative in the state Assembly for several sessions. Anderson encouraged Earl to point toward the district attorney's office in Alameda County as the best place in the state to garner experience, since this office, unlike those in other communities, handled both the civil as well as criminal work of the county. He offered to recommend Earl to District Attorney Ezra Decoto.

When Decoto came up to Sacramento from Oakland to have the legislature authorize the employment of another man in his district attorney's office, the legislators made their first gesture toward "veteran's aid."

"We'd be delighted, Mr. Decoto, only that extra man you want to employ will have to be Earl Warren."

Decoto protested that he already had a man selected, one who had been trained for the job. The legislators were adamant about their "aid bill." "Sorry," they said, "it's Warren or nobody."

When Earl Warren learned of this he went directly to Decoto, whom he had never met before, and said, "Mr. Decoto, I want you to know that I've had nothing to do with the effort to force my services on you. I'd like nothing better than to work in your office, but I couldn't take the job under these circumstances. You just go ahead and hire your own man; I won't take the job."

Decoto was grateful. "I appreciate that, Warren. If there should ever be an opening in the district attorney's office, I'll keep you in mind."

At the end of three months when the legislature completed its session, Warren returned to Oakland, bought a civilian suit out of his Sacramento earnings, and arranged to share offices with Leon Gray in the Bank of Italy building. Gray also worked as a deputy city attorney for Oakland, and before a private client managed to find his way into Lawyer Warren's office, a vacancy arose in the office of the city attorney, H. L. Hagan. Hagan offered Warren the job at two hundred dollars a month, with the right to practice law on the side.

"It didn't take me long to make up my mind," says Warren. "I didn't want money. I only wanted the right kind of experience. For the past nine years, ever since I entered Boalt Hall, I had been looking for the chance to get practical experience; now at last the heavy gate was opening for me."

The next seven months were exciting ones for Warren, for in addition to his research in this new field of civic government, he had plenty of opportunity to write opinions for city department heads who wanted to be advised on their powers, and on proper procedure. He also went into court to defend the city and its officials in civil litigation. He was far too interested in his new job to seek private clients.

His only unhappiness arose from the illness of Frank Anderson who had been stricken with tuberculosis and was confined to his bed. Though his strength was failing fast, Frank told Earl that he was anxious to file his statement of candidacy for re-election to the legislature. Warren learned from the doctor that his friend had no chance, but both men agreed that they could not break his wonderful spirit.

When he called on Frank that night, and Anderson insisted that he would soon be well, Earl said, "Frank, if you feel that way, let's get the papers filed and start with the campaign." Since he knew little about election procedures, he asked the Oakland newspapermen what he should do. He then staged press conferences at his friend's bedside, and the newspapermen pitched in to help. On election day, when Warren went from polling booth to polling booth, he saw that Anderson was running behind in the tally. By midnight Frank's friends gave up and went home; Earl was too heartbroken to go home, but plodded through the hours and the deserted streets, still haunting the polling booths, wondering how he could break this bad news to Frank.

Toward morning he at last came to the two most populous precincts. Here, as he watched over the teller's shoulder in the dim light of the smoking kerosene lamps, he saw that Frank was overcoming his opponent's lead. At dawn, Anderson emerged triumphant—by thirty-five votes! There were no streetcars running at this hour, so Earl walked the several miles to the Anderson house, knocking on Frank's window just as the sun rose. The sick man was overjoyed at the news, and the two friends sat for several hours over steaming cups of coffee, discussing politics and Earl Warren's first contact with the active mechanics of a campaign and an election.

Frank Anderson died two days later. He died happy, and with Earl Warren's name on his lips.

V. Work and Love

ON MAY 1, 1920, Ezra Decoto at last had a vacancy for a deputy in his office. During the past months he and Warren had frequently worked together on problems of civil law, and Decoto had developed a respect for the younger man's energy and enthusiasm. He offered Earl the deputy's job at a hundred and fifty dollars a month. It can rightly be said that Warren's career began at this instant, though he could not foresee its outline.

"Once again I saw the opportunity to get the experience I wanted. The drop in salary bothered me not at all. I thought I would work in the district attorney's office for about a year and a half, and at the end of that time I would go into private practice and become a great trial lawyer. So I worked sixteen hours a day for the first five years, and ended up by remaining eighteen years, often working until midnight at least five nights a week."

Alameda County, with its almost half-million population, was the third largest in the state, surpassed only by San Francisco and Los Angeles. It combined nine cities and towns including the sprawling seaports of Oakland and Alameda; as the western terminus for the three transcontinental railroads, the Southern Pacific, the Western Pacific, and the Sante Fe, it had become one of the great railroad centers of the United States. In terms of geography it comprised seven hundred and thirty-three square miles, which made it about two-thirds as large as Rhode Island. It also contained the state university at Berkeley which, with its ten thousand students, was the largest in the world. In addition to its shipping and railroad activities, it was a large industrial center with factories spread along the Bay coast of Berkeley, Emeryville and Oakland, all of it backed up by large agricultural acreage and population.

The County Courthouse to which Warren now moved his briefcase was an antiquated two-and-a-half-story wooden structure on Broadway, between Third and Fourth Streets, in a neighborhood which had long ceased to be Oakland's most desirable. In the early morning he walked up the wide wooden staircase to the second floor, and then proceeded to his own cubbyhole, which was exactly like the tiny offices of all the other deputies. Ever since entering law school, he had been complaining silently at the insufficient work and action. Now he had enough action to satisfy a dozen men, for it was the era of the bootlegger, rumrunner, hijacker, crooked gambler, hired killer, of gang warfare, protection rackets, smuggling, dope and prostitution rings, of flaming youth, and the enormously prosperous alliance between government and crime—not on as large a scale as Thomas E. Dewey would soon face in New York, but still of such

formidable proportion as to intimidate the local government and large segments of the population. Not since
the gold rush days of 1849, before the state had any
government at all, had there been such widespread and
powerful disregard of the law and its enforcement officers. To Warren, sections of Alameda County in which
he was now to meet his first and vigorous test resembled
nothing so much as the wild and lawless Bakersfield of
his own youth. Despite Methias and Crystal Warren's
uneasiness, their son had been raised in exactly the right
environment!

Ezra Decoto had been appointed district attorney
by the Alameda Board of Supervisors in 1916, and then
been elected to two four-year terms by the voters. He
was a kindly, judicious man who ran a thoroughly honest
office; he was not a militant law-enforcement officer.
Decoto was practicing curative law, but not preventive
law: he prosecuted well the criminal cases which came
into his office; he investigated unsavory conditions
whenever a complaint was filed. He did not go out
looking for criminal rings, racketeers or combinations
between the underworld and city officials, for he had an
insufficient number of deputies to handle the complaints
and prosecutions already in the district attorney's office.
The legal codes and court procedures were a full genera-
tion behind the modern, streamlined criminal structure
of the new age. Even if Ezra Decoto had wanted to be
a crusader he would have found little encouragement
and less help from the apathetic residents and from the
businessmen who wanted things kept quiet so that Alameda County would not get a bad name.

However, Decoto's greatest weakness was a lack of talent for organization. A case that came into the office was handed over to the deputy who had just finished his last assignment. No one else in the office knew what the case was about, what stage of progress it might be in, or what kind of evidence had been gathered. Since the deputies received miserably low wages, and had to find a sufficient number of outside cases to support their families, it was impossible to set up standards or time schedules. As a result, cases frequently dragged on so long that the evidence and witnesses vanished, the public lost what interest it might have had in the beginning, and the complainant dropped his charges through sheer weariness.

Most of the deputies had already been in the office for some ten years when Warren entered. They were growing a little stale; in addition they were taking all of the outside practice they could possibly get. There was a financial boom at the moment, and there was a great deal of money to be made in private law; many of the older deputies were laying their plans to resign. Under such conditions their hearts and minds would be more on the future than on the remnants of cases left on their hands. If this did not work to the county's advantage, it certainly did to Deputy Warren's: he was a bachelor, his parents needed no financial help, nor was he yet interested in romance. The romance in his life was the Law, and no woman ever got a more passionate rush from an excited admirer than did the Alameda County district attorney's office from Earl Warren. It was not only exactly the right place for young Warren, but it was also exactly the right time.

When he joined the district attorney's staff he threw
away the clock and the calendar. He was avid not only
for the experience he so badly needed, but for knowledge
as well. There was nothing taking place in the office
which did not stimulate his eager mind. He did not
intrude, but wherever a deputy wanted to discuss a
case or was seeking help or was grateful for assistance in
reading a thick file, Warren was on hand. There were
few secrets in the office, or personal rivalries, and since
he had already been acquainted with most of the deputies before entering the district attorney's office, he enjoyed working friendships with them. A likable young
man who has endless energy, who is willing to help in
any tedious or laborious phase of a case, to stay up until
midnight or until dawn to help prepare material, and
listen with complete attention and respect to the work-
ings of other men's minds; who is not anxious to mani-
fest his own brightness, wisdom, skill or superiority, is
not trying to steal anybody's job, get publicity, or in-
dulge in ego bolstering—such a young man would
naturally be the recipient of a good deal of accumula-
tive wisdom, and would be admitted to the inside of as
many cases in the office as the hours of the day would
permit.

Decoto says, "When Earl Warren came into my office
as a deputy, I would frequently ask him on Saturday
morning if he could find me some law on a case in the
office in the course of the next few days. Monday
morning there would invariably be a memorandum on
my desk setting forth all the law on the subject involved."

Whenever a deputy would move out into private

practice, and this was happening every few weeks now, Decoto would exclaim:

"My God, who knows anything about his cases?"

Someone around the office would invariably reply, "Well, Warren does," and with a profound sense of relief Decoto would put these cases on Warren's already high-piled desk.

All of the years of instinctive feeling he had had about the law now came into focus for Earl Warren. The fifteen-hour day was a joy and a challenge rather than a burden; he worked until midnight and past, his only recreation having dinner in downtown Oakland with one or two of the younger men in the office or his former Boalt Hall friends who were in private practice. He was wise enough not to neglect his health, and in warm weather he would go down to Schmidt's Cottage Baths in Alameda where he would take a quick swim in the bay, then have a milkshake and sandwich before returning to the office at the end of his lunch hour. On Sunday afternoon he played baseball with a group of amateurs, mostly old friends from college, at the Municipal Playgrounds. If he had a particularly grueling night's work ahead, he would play handball for a half hour at the Athens Athletic Club or the Elks Club before his dinner.

Though he went to an occasional party, dance or picnic on the weekend, and met attractive young women, he was still a long way from becoming serious about love or marriage. He wanted to establish himself and be sure what he was going to do with his future before he undertook a family of his own. Being a bachelor was considerably simplified for him by the fact that he had a good home with his sister Ethel, had a fine friendship with his brother-in-law Vernon, and was devoted to his eight-year-old niece Dorothy, and his one-year-old nephew Warren. The finest tribute he could have paid to his parents was his great love of children; and he knew that once he married he wanted to have at least half a dozen. But in the meanwhile the normal irritations which drive the single man to marry: the monotonous food in the restaurants, the buttons that are missing from shirts, the loneliness of a hotel room when one feels in a conversational mood, all these were eliminated by the Planks' adoption of him into their rambling home as a member of the family. He was not inclined to experiment with a dozen love affairs before finding a wife by the trial-and-error method; he felt that at the proper time he would meet the one right woman for him, that they would love and marry.

One soft spring morning he was invited to a Sunday birthday breakfast given by a young married couple. The guests met at nine o'clock to swim at the Piedmont Baths. Earl got into his suit, walked from the locker room to the deep end of the plunge, greeted a number of his friends, then looked out toward the pool where there was a good deal of friendly splashing and laughter. There he saw a face: and momentarily his world stopped. The young woman was in water up to her shoulders, a bathing cap covering all but the oval of her face. He could not tear his gaze away from the enormous eyes, fair skin, rosy cheeks which were just the right touch on the plump side, the full rich mouth and well modeled chin. Somewhere from out of his past, from deep in his unconscious memory, from the gallery of thousands of pictures, from the realm of the wish unfulfilled and the hope yet to come, voices spoke to him, the fragments whirled and settled into a whole, this one face came up to him out of the water, life-size, breathing, lovely, resolving all that had gone before and everything that was to come.

He turned to his hostess and said, "Would you . . . would you please . . . introduce me?"

Nina Palmquist had looked up from the water and seen Earl Warren at the very instant that he had seen her. Her hostess came toward her. The introductions were made in a low voice. Earl saw that her eyes were not only large but wondrously alive and expressive. With their first murmured words of greeting, their first handclasp, their first swift and deep probing into each other's eyes, Earl Warren's old life ended and his new life began.

The story of Nina Palmquist's family follows with remarkable coincidence the story of the older Warrens. Nina had been born in Sweden and brought to Iowa when she was an infant, just as Crystal Warren had been. Then her parents had gone west to San Diego searching for a warm dry climate because of delicate health. Here, when Nina was only three, her mother died in childbirth. Brokenhearted, her father took his three young daughters, Eva, Nina and Hannah, and moved north to Oakland, hoping to flood out his memories and find a new life. But he had not been the kind of man who could begin anew; instead he married an older woman, one whom Nina had described as a noble soul, in order that his children might be cared for. The stepmother gave them a full bounty of love and devotion; but the father never found health or happiness again, and died of tuberculosis when Nina was only thirteen. He left no resources behind him.

Nina's older sister, Eva, worked for the large plumbing supply house of Willis B. George. Nina sometimes stopped off to visit with her sister, and Eva devoted a few spare moments to showing the younger girl how she kept her set of books. The University of California, where Earl Warren had spent six delightful years, was only a short streetcar ride away, but to Nina it may as well have been in another world, for when she finished school she had to go to work. She enrolled at the Healds Business College. At this point the Crane Company fixture salesman who handled the Willis B. George account, and who had watched Eva manage the office, offered her a far better job with the Crane Company. Eva went to her employer and told him of her opportunity. George said, "All right, I won't stand in your way, but I've seen you showing the ropes to that young sister of yours, so suppose you train her to take over before you leave."

Nina went to work as a cashier and bookkeeper for Mr. George and continued her stenographic course at Healds in the night classes. Since there were several short periods during the day when she was not busy she asked her boss if she could study her shorthand during this spare time. Mr. George replied, "Certainly not!" If she had any spare time it would be much better if she went back into the stockroom and acquainted herself with the fittings. Instead of being offended, Nina did as she was told; to her surprise she found that she was "fascinated by all the thousands of different small items, each in its cubbyhole, just as neat and tidy as possible. I went back to the storeroom so often that after a while I learned the business very well, and that was good for me."

Once again the Crane salesman raided Willis B. George, saying to Nina, "How would you like to work with Eva in our Oakland office?" In the meanwhile, young Hannah had been stopping by on her way home to visit with Nina, and Nina had continued the family tradition. When she went to Mr. George to tell him that she too was being offered a better opportunity by Crane, the resigned gentleman said, "All right, but bring that young sister of yours in here and teach her to take over your job."

In the meantime Nina had completed her course at Healds Business College and she and Eva had given young Hannah a thorough business training. Before long the three Palmquist girls were managing the Crane offices in Oakland and San Francisco, moving about almost interchangeably, earning good salaries, liked and respected in the business community. Then Eva married a graduate from the Christian Bible Institute and went with him to China, where they served as missionaries for twenty years. Nina married a musician, Grover Meyers. Shortly after, Hannah married a railroad engineer.

The dread curse of tuberculosis soon turned bright and fun-loving young Nina's life to tragedy: her husband came down with the then incurable disease, and died when Nina's son was only three weeks old.

These were difficult times for the young girl, but she faced them with resolution. She went back to live with her stepmother, knowing that she would have to find employment to support her boy. A few weeks later, when she was wheeling young Jim in his baby carriage, a sympathetic neighbor stopped to talk, asking what she intended to do. Nina said she hadn't yet decided. The woman, who owned a specialty shop which sold a fine line of women's clothing, lingerie and hosiery, offered Nina a job, saying, "You will owe me money at first, but I'm willing to take a chance on you."

Nina went to work with a vengeance. After only a few weeks she had proved herself so capable that the owner raised her wages. A few months later the woman bought a second shop, and made Nina manager of the first one. At the end of a year the owner had acquired a third shop, and Nina had done so well that she was made manager of the small chain.

Nina worked hard, not only because she had to earn money to pay for Jim's keep and for insurance so that he would be protected if anything happened to her, but because she loved merchandising; it gave her an interest and a way of life. She went out not at all, but rose early, gave little Jim his breakfast, and was at the largest of the three shops, only five blocks from home, by seven in the morning. The owner didn't want her to wait on customers, thinking that it was beneath her manager's dignity, but Nina loved to meet people, and so she opened the street doors at eight o'clock and would write up a full book of sales before the regular salespeople arrived at nine. At six o'clock she went home to have dinner with Jim, played with him for an hour, read him a story and then tucked him in bed. With the child asleep, Nina would go back to the store to work until midnight. She hoped that within a few years she would be able to open a shop of her own, thus earning security for herself and her boy.

This was the young woman whom Earl Warren now saw standing before him, a woman with courage and character, sensitivity and beauty all discernible in her lovely face. Nor did it do any serious injury to Warren's benumbed feelings that she also had a fine figure.

As she felt her hand crushed in Warren's, felt the great warmth of his smile and the openness of his personality, as she sensed the deep-rooted integrity of the man, Nina too knew that the past was irretrievably gone and that the future stretched ahead, good and beautiful.

"I spotted him just as quickly as he spotted me."

Though there were twenty guests at the party, Warren managed to get himself seated next to Nina. She was wearing a black dress which set off her blond hair to its best advantage. They talked animatedly through the entire breakfast. As they parted he asked if he could see her the following Saturday. He took her to the Fulton Stock Company in Oakland, where they watched *Smilin' Through* and later, *Rose of the Rancho*. After that they went out together every Saturday night, either to see a play, or dinner-dancing. They had little time for each other during the week for, as Nina Warren says, "I was as busy at my job as he was at his." Nina devoted all day Sunday to her son, and Earl, who had joined the Sequoia Golf Club, was trying to break ninety.

Warren never talked about his work to Nina. He had no wish to discuss during his few free hours the sordid panorama of human weakness, venality, brutality and destruction which passed before his eyes in the district attorney's office. Further, he did not believe that Nina should be burdened with this nether-side of human life. When they were together he wanted them to establish their own common ground for fun, and companionship, so that when he was released from his work he could turn to her for relaxation and they could enjoy the simple, unburdened pleasures of young people in love.

With the older deputies resigning apace, he moved up quickly. At the end of his prescribed year and a half he felt that he had accumulated only the smallest part of the skill he desired, that he was making such rapid progress in the office he ought to stay and play the game out. But the major reason he wanted to remain was his realization that under its present setup the district attorney's office was accomplishing about ten percent of its potential, and letting the other ninety percent go by default, a default shared by the county, state and federal governments.

Every district attorney's office throughout the state was an island unto itself; racketeers, criminals and swindlers operated in one county until they were on the verge of being caught, then moved a few miles north or south to continue their depredations without molestation. Every police force was an island unto itself, there was no connection with any other community, and no cooperation between them on their common problems. No community kept a complete record of its crimes, nor did it have any way of knowing the past record of the criminals with whom it had to deal. A burglar operating in Alameda County might have been convicted on any number of charges in a dozen other states, but since there was no national file of identification, each district attorney had to begin at scratch and hope to ferret out the criminal's past from his unwilling lips.

The county was run by the Mike Kelly machine, and political appointments and nominations were granted on the basis of party service. Some of the city and county councils, police chiefs, sheriffs, and a good many of the policemen were in partnership with bootleggers, bond brokers, dope peddlers, swindlers, thieves, procurers, rum runners, gamblers and the whole retinue of petty criminals who thronged into Alameda because of the soft pickings and the protection they could get from some law-enforcement officers. The public was indifferent to the constant stream of small crimes that went on in the county. Even a man who was robbed, and screamed for justice, quickly forgot his grievance when the insurance company had paid his claim. The big-time gangster was glamorized in Alameda County, with his picture on the front pages of the newspapers and everyone thrilled by his exploits. When a convicted bank robber and habitual criminal escaped from San Quentin, Warren asked every businessman he met in Oakland what he thought about the escape; he was amazed to find that many law-abiding citizens were hoping the police did not catch him, for the bank robber had fired their imaginations, and become a hero.

If the district attorney's office made an attempt to arrest rumrunners or bootleggers, the public said, "Aw, let them alone, we don't like the prohibition law, and we want our liquor." The men who ran houses in Emeryville, or sold liquor on the high-school grounds, or opened crooked gambling joints, were considered to be small businessmen trying to get along in the world and affording the county a little innocent pleasure. The public had no way of knowing that most of these profits sifted upward to their officials, spread corruption throughout their local government; or if they knew, they didn't care, because times were good and everyone was making a living. If the district attorney's office made an arrest, spent months in the gathering of evidence and the preparation of the trial, and did secure a conviction, the money of the underworld and the influence of the ring officials was exerted upon the Parole Board to get them released and brought back into the main stream of the county's crime structure.

To Earl Warren this seemed not only a travesty of justice, but a perversion of good government, wasteful of the life, funds, and safety of the community, and growing at such an accelerated rate that before long the criminal ring would control the entire county.

The talent for organization seems to be born in a person; it is sometimes merely the need of an orderly mind trying to project itself. Warren's gift manifested itself late, when he was past thirty, but then he had matured late, physically, mentally and even emotionally.

He now found in himself a need to see things sensibly and efficiently organized, a need which arose out of the distress which his neat soul, for Methias and Crystal were orderly and disciplined spirits, suffered in this haphazard office.

He knew that he wanted to tackle the district attorney's job. He could wait. One day his chief would move on to a kind of work which better suited his gifts and temperament, and then he would announce his intentions. One of his main qualities, possibly a result of his Scandinavian heritage, is that he is never in such a tearing, blinding hurry that he will violate his own loyalties, break relationships, or disrupt an office.

He says, "A man should never be in a hurry for a political job; when he starts pushing, he thinks and does things he would never do under normal circumstances."

There was time; neither he, the job, nor America would blow away in the first windstorm; and it was better to pick the fruit in season. This patience and waiting would prove a recurrent pattern in Earl Warren's career.

As he now moved into every nook and cranny of Alameda County, securing documentary evidence on the overall web of crime and corruption, he began almost unconsciously to plan the kind of organization that would be needed to clean it up and make the community a beautiful place in which to live.

The first task would be somehow to arouse the public, enlist the support of stout-hearted groups who would stand by him in the pinches. Then he would have to hire additional deputies from among the recent graduates of the best law colleges, men who were as hungry for experience as he had been when he graduated from Boalt Hall. He would have to reorganize the office so that every deputy became a specialist, better trained and more able in court than the lawyers used by the criminal rings; and he would have to pay them enough salary so they could devote their full time, energy and loyalty to the task.

The antiquated legal codes would have to be sharply overhauled, the court procedures revised so that the community might have an even chance with the law breaker. He would have to accumulate slowly and patiently the evidence and documentation on the tie-up between the county's criminals and the law-enforcement offices, then persuade the newspapers, business community and the grand jury to face the seriousness of the situation. He would have to evolve a technique of going into court with such incontrovertible cases that he would make Alameda County an unhealthy place for the predatory. Lastly, he would have to fight for a revised conception of the parole laws so that the office would not have the identical criminals to prosecute each time they came back from lunch.

Once he had formulated these plans he redoubled his efforts in the office and the courts. In 1923 Decoto named him his chief deputy. Then came his most important assignment, and the one which led swiftly to the realization of his dreams: Decoto appointed his chief deputy to serve as legal counsel to the County Board of Supervisors. Warren continued with the major portion of his criminal and civil work inside the district attorney's office, but in addition he sat with the board of supervisors in order to give them legal opinions on their official actions, such as purchases, the construction of public works, and passing of new ordinances. He also handled the civil litigation which involved the board. He became well acquainted with one of the supervisors, Johnny Mullins, a delightful and affectionate Irishman who developed a strong attachment to him.

An old classmate of Warren's believes that Decoto purposely assigned Warren as counsel for the board of supervisors knowing that he, Decoto, was soon going to resign and be appointed to a state commission, and thus Warren would have the inside track on the remainder of the term as district attorney. The fact remains that the inside track was a bit muddy: of the five members of the board, three, including Mullins, were Kelly men, elected by the machine. Kelly and Warren were not friends.

A short time later the rumors about Decoto were confirmed; the governor named him to the Railroad Commission. Encountering Warren in the courthouse, Mike Kelly said, "Warren, I have nothing against you personally. My only objection to your being appointed to fill out the term is that you have not earned it politically. I have promised it to Frank Shay, whose friends have been my supporters for years."

"Mr. Kelly, you can't expect me to withdraw from the contest just because you've promised it to someone else."

"I can understand your wanting the job, all right," said Kelly, "but it's futile for you to expect to receive it."

Warren announced himself for the district attorney's job. When one of Kelly's men assured him of his support, he decided he was in. A few days later a friend informed him that the vote was two to two, with Mullins' the deciding vote.

Warren was disappointed: for Mullins alone to defy the Kelly machine would be the Oakland version of hara-kiri. That afternoon Johnny Mullins came into the office and after a stumbling introduction said, "Earl, the minute I leave here I am going out to tell every man in this community whose respect I value, every doctor, lawyer and businessman, that I am going to vote for you for district attorney when the time comes. Then it will be just impossible for even Mike Kelly to make me change my mind."

Johnny Mullins stuck to his word. The board of supervisors by a vote of three to two appointed Earl Warren District Attorney of Alameda County. The Kelly machine ousted Mullins from the board of supervisors the following year, and to this day Johnny Mullins swears that it was worth the price.

Earl and Nina celebrated his appointment by being married in Oakland. They went north to Vancouver for a leisurely honeymoon, then returned to Oakland where they lived in a hotel for a few months until they located a pleasant flat on Greenwood Avenue. Warren came home each night for dinner, but afterwards he returned to his office or attended important meetings. They continued the pattern they had set of keeping their extremely happy personal life completely divorced from Earl's professional life.

"I had worked so much myself," says Nina Warren, "that I knew how a person felt when he came home at night, tired."

Nina Warren created a beautiful home for her husband and Jim, whom Earl had adopted, one in which he always found peace, comradeship, a warm welcoming smile, complete ease and security. These qualities deepened with the passage of the years and the coming of the other Warren children.

"We decided that we wanted six youngsters," says Mrs. Warren, "three girls for Earl, and three boys for me."

As district attorney Warren quickly divided his task into four categories: the prosecution of individual crimes against persons or property; of organized and conspiratorial crimes against large numbers of persons; of crimes against the state; and the remedial work, the throwing out of obsolete and senseless laws, the departmentalization of the office, and the awakening and educating of the public so that it would know how completely the community had been corrupted.

First he endeavored to bring the calendar up to date and to dispose of those elemental cases in the initial category which he had inherited from Decoto: the jealous husband who had killed a man allegedly paying attention to his wife; the unmarried girl who had disposed of her infant; the doctor who was charged with statutory offenses; the crimes of stickup men, second-story men, bank robbers.

After that he tackled the bail-bond racket which had grown so powerful that it was about to devour the police courts. The runners were always on hand, working with the clerks, sheriffs and police. If a defendant dug into his pocket to put up his bail, the cash was refused; he was told that he would have to employ the bail-bond company. So arrogant had the ring become that the bail-bond runners paid the clerks and other court officials their rake-off right in front of the victim. The Alameda brokers were resourceful men who had built their racket into high finance: when working people got into trouble the bail-bond companies would take their homes as security, but so strong was their influence that they could keep getting a case postponed, with the interest charges mounting, until the accused had lost his home. Where criminals jumped their bail the bonding companies connived with officials to have the cases set aside or postponed. By this series of devices the bail-bond companies put up no cash, nor did they have to forfeit a bond even when the culprit skipped town.

Warren called the bail-bond brokers into his office and warned them that if they did not cease these activities he would indict them. A few of the smaller brokers heeded his notice, but Meyers and Company, which had secured a monopoly on about ninety percent of the bail-bond business, laughed outright at this young innocent.

"Take it easy, District Attorney, you'll live longer."

Warren had no intention of taking it easy: he watched Meyers, saw that he was disregarding the warning, then started to build his case. Friends and well-wishers said:

"Earl, you can't do this. You have to stand for election in a few months, and they will smear your name so badly that you won't have a chance."

He answered, "I took an oath to enforce the law, and I will."

He went over the court records, got the names and addresses of hundreds of people who had dealt with Meyers, and soon had them in his office relating their pathetic stories. Warren's prosecution of Meyers was his first great test against organized crime.

"I decided to stay in public service the minute the pressures were applied against me: pressures applied by bail bondsmen, gamblers, petty thieves, swindlers and politicians. I then realized for the first time what public service could mean. That is when I decided to stay with it."

He went into court with a tremendous bulk of evidence, and a long string of the injured as witnesses. He indulged in no forensics or showmanship; he played no tricks, did not wave his arms or shout. Frank Coakley, the present District Attorney of Alameda County, says, "Earl Warren was excellent in both the civil and criminal fields of law. Before a jury and judge he was very fair but firm, and a vigorous cross-examiner. If a man was lying, it was too bad for him. His courtroom manner was able and workmanlike. He never missed any bets, but covered all the bags." He was quiet, relentlessly logical, building up such a tight case that the bail-bond ring was effectively smashed.

He subpoenaed the court records, and this time made the brokers pay over to the state all bonds that had been forfeited, and secured the return of property which had been mulcted from the public. Bail-bond abuses disappeared from Alameda, and the brokers thereafter contented themselves with the legal rates of interest.

He had been in office only a little over a year when the general elections came around. "I managed to win that election," he says, "by meeting and talking to more voters than any candidate had ever talked to before." He was opposed by a deputy district attorney who had been in the office with him, but his work had won him an opening wedge of confidence. He was elected for a four-year term with more votes than all the other candidates put together.

VI. Baptism by Fire

WHEN he was sworn into office Earl Warren said, "I will enforce the law strictly and uniformly."

The poison and the antidote are so often created together. At that same election, in November of 1926, there was elected as Sheriff of Alameda County, and the man with whom District Attorney Warren would have to work in the closest alliance, the former Piedmont police chief, Burton F. Becker. The Sheriff was not a man to let any grass grow under his feet: between his election in November, and his induction in January, 1927, Becker, his campaign manager, and the bosses of the underworld who had contributed so much to elect him, organized one of the tightest graft rings ever forged on the Pacific Coast, tying in every still operator, bootlegger, crooked gambler, marihuana, dope and flesh peddler in the county. On the day that Sheriff Becker took his oath of office, the rolls of greenbacks held together with rubber bands began to change hands.

On that same day, with the evidence of these transactions reaching him with almost the directness of a pistol shot, the new District Attorney knew that the conditions during the past few years were going to seem like the peccadillos of naughty children compared to what he would have to face under the new regime. Before Becker had been sheriff one month the scandal began to smell worse than the marshes down around Emeryville.

Warren called Becker in and told him what he knew of the bootlegging, crooked gambling, prostitution and bunko games, and then advised him to clean up his office. Becker replied good-naturedly that he certainly would do so.

During the second month the stench grew stronger. Warren repeated his warning. A few weeks later he told Becker that he had gone as far as any good neighbor should, that he couldn't continue these warnings without losing his self-respect.

"You take care of the district attorney's office," replied Becker grimly, "and I'll take care of myself."

Still hoping to clean up the mess quietly, Warren then asked Richard Carrington, publisher of the Oakland *Post-Inquirer*, to invite Mike Kelly to his office for a conference. In the presence of the newspaperman Warren told Kelly, who had backed Becker's election, that the sheriff was continuing to house the rackets in his official capacity, and that if he did not clean house, the district attorney's office would be obliged to step in and do so. Also that he would do everything possible to get the evidence with which to indict him.

"Mr. Kelly, I don't want you to believe that politics is or ever will be my motive. That's the reason I'm telling you beforehand of the situation."

"Thank you, Mr. District Attorney. I will talk to

Becker and tell him that he must get along with you, and that if he doesn't, he needn't look to me for help." The next day Kelly said, "I have talked to Becker. He has promised to go straight and cooperate in the enforcement of the law."

Becker was kidding. Warren had asked the sheriff to pass along his warning to his deputies; now, fearful lest this had not been done, and wanting to give everyone a chance to fulfill his own job, he summoned each of Becker's deputies to his office. To one deputy, he said,

"Shurtleff, you have eight children, and the last thing in the world I want to do is send a man to San Quentin who has eight kids to support. For the sake of those youngsters, why don't you go straight?"

Shurtleff replied arrogantly, "If you think you've got anything on me, go ahead and prosecute," then turned his back and walked out.

District Attorney Warren became of necessity a muckraker, and in the fuzzy mind of the public it sometimes seemed as though he were the one creating the muck. The business community and many of its leading citizens were appalled at what Warren had turned up, making it evident that they wished he would quiet down, take his job philosophically, and not bring so much unfavorable publicity upon their heads. Half of his time he devoted to fighting the criminals on the bottom rung of society and the other half to waking the top rung from its apathy. Every day at lunch and as often as five nights a week he attended meetings of the Rotarians, the Lions, the American Legion posts, the teachers' associations, the bar and medical associations, the forums, the women's clubs, the Knights of the Round Table, the Councils of Jewish Women, the chambers of commerce, talking to them about crime, showing them the extent to which combinations of the underworld and their civic government now squandered their taxes, corrupted their public services and made life unsafe in the county. He startled his audiences by telling them, and proving, that there were more murders committed in Alameda County each year than in London, a city of ten millions; that more felons were given probation in Alameda County than were given jail sentences; that businessmen who would not tolerate for a moment a gang hovering around their employees for the purpose of making them unfaithful to their employers, permitted the bootleggers, dope peddlers and petty criminals to hang around and influence the employees of the state.

"The government is a business," said Warren, "and the integrity of those who carry it on is important. But for some reason keeping the business of local government up to the standard of private business is considered reform."

He joined the American Legion, Elks, Native Sons, Moose and Exchange Club, working actively within these groups, making friends for his concept of good government. In the big cases he had to secure grand jury indictments before he could get the culprits into court; and so he had to persuade the solid element in the county not only to serve on the grand jury at considerable sacrifice of their time and interest, but also to back up the grand jury indictments once they were secured.

He devoted more and more time and care to the selection of his deputies. "I surrounded myself with young Boalt Hall graduates who were seeking experience. When

I had no opening for them in the district attorney's office, they took unpaid deputy jobs. The moment there was an opening they became members of the staff."

He placed less emphasis upon grades, for he still remembered his own difficulties at Boalt Hall, than upon character, native intelligence, willingness to sacrifice to the task on hand, and as important as any of these the man's family life: whether he was stable emotionally, would find sympathy at home with the rigorous demands of the job, and above all be able to resist the tremendous temptations of easy money and easy pleasure with which the underworld tries to bribe officials.

He helped create the pattern: though he had enjoyed a glass of beer and, in particular, a bourbon and soda with friends before dinner, the moment the Volstead Act was passed he became a teetotaler.

"How can I drink bootleg liquor at a party on Sunday night, and then on Monday morning send my deputies to prosecute bootleggers?"

Most of his deputies followed his example, knowing that they were protecting the district attorney's office.

The office settled down to a rigorously organized but thoroughly creative approach to the problem of law enforcement. Warren divided the staff into five departments; each morning at eight-thirty he met with a different department for an hour, during which they would thrash out their difficulties. At closing time, when the telephones were shut off and the front door locked, he remained behind to work with the deputies who were involved in complicated cases and wanted discussion or counsel.

Frank Coakley says, "Warren was a prodigious worker. Time never meant anything to him when there was a job to be done. For some of our cases we were in court three or four months; after leaving the courtroom we'd go back to the office and work all night to prepare for the next day, taking just enough time off to go home for a shower and breakfast."

On Saturday morning at eight-thirty the entire office gathered to correlate the week's work, informing each other of progress and results on the one hand, of complications and failure on the other. Every man's problem, both personal and professional, became the common problem of the entire staff.

Warren would caution the men, "Let's look at this thing, let's get the facts straight, and settle this in the public interest. You cannot unring a bell. What you do you have to live with. We may get hurt for a while, but we can live with this, we can be comfortable with it."

The deputies called him Chief, and he was at all times the chief executive of the office; but just as he was arbitrary in his demands that the corrupt officials and rings be prosecuted, to the same extent he was open, friendly and receptive to every word offered him by a deputy district attorney. Every man in the office had the right to speak his mind, down to the youngest and newest deputy: a right to express his opinion of the way cases were being handled, the validity of briefs and opinions and the general techniques of the office.

"If it is a mistake of the head and not the heart," said Warren, "don't worry about it, that's the way we learn."

"He set the example himself," said Coakley. "He did everything in good taste, was calm and cool. Neither

he nor anyone else in the office resorted to showmanship
or tricks, or the flamboyant manner of the old-time lawyers. If for any reason we let him down, we caught the
devil, but that was the end of it. He never carried anything over. A fine spirit of loyalty and comradeship
developed in the office."

Others of the deputies say, "We shared friendship, confidence, devotion, work. If anyone needed money, all of
our funds were available to him. When there was sick-
ness in a deputy's family we made him stay home or at
the hospital, and took over his work. When anyone had
a birthday there was a big party in the office after hours."
Helen MacGregor, a Boalt Hall graduate who has been
Warren's personal secretary over all the years, declares,
"It was the closest thing to blood brothership many of
us had ever known."

Despite this closeness of relationship every man's rights
were rigorously protected. In 1928 when Warren was a
leader of the Alameda County Republican Party's campaign for Herbert Hoover, a local politician said, "Look,
this is an embarrassing situation: you are head of the
Hoover-for-President movement, and one of your deputies is taking an important part in the Al Smith campaign. That doesn't make sense."

"The district attorney's office is nonpartisan," replied
Warren. "If Frank Coakley thinks Al Smith should be
elected, he has every right to devote his spare time to the
Democratic candidate."

He gave every man his head, reposing full confidence
in his ability and integrity, a confidence that was never
violated. During his thirteen years as district attorney
and four years as attorney general, with as many as fifty

deputies under him, no member of Earl Warren's staff was ever involved in a scandal, personal or professional.

This same trust and confidence he extended to those coming in contact with the district attorney's office, and to the people who ran afoul of the law. He went to Willard Shea, the public defender, who was a man of the highest integrity, and whose duty it was to represent those who had no funds with which to hire private counsel.

"Willard, I know that you don't want to keep guilty men out of jail any more than I want to put innocent ones in. Therefore, I will make an agreement with you: if at any time you are convinced that we have indicted an innocent man, just come and tell me so. I will then show you my files on the case. If after looking over my material you are still convinced that the man is innocent, I will release him."

About once a year, Public Defender Shea would come to District Attorney Warren and declare that a certain client was innocent. If Warren's material couldn't change Shea's mind, the District Attorney released the prisoner. Occasionally Shea would come into the office and exclaim, "You are giving my client a rough time, and I think that such and such should be done." Warren would say with a little smile, "Willard, you know our agreement: are you prepared to tell me that this man is innocent?" Shea would exclaim, "Oh, go to hell!" and leave the office.

Shea, who is still the public defender in Oakland, says, "Warren never brought people into court until he was positive they were guilty and could prove it. He would always discuss a case with me before going into court, rather than keeping his evidence secret so he could spring it before a jury and thus upset or weaken my defense. I tried a number of cases against Warren, but I never won one."

Then Shea adds with a sad, wistful smile, "But of course my defendants were never innocent."

He was not out to secure the greatest number of convictions. Frank Coakley, then Warren's chief deputy, says:

"When I worked on a case and sometimes found something to give me a reasonable doubt, I'd tell Warren, and he'd say, 'If that's the way you feel about it, let's dismiss the case.'"

There were three cases of rape in quick succession in Oakland, all of them committed by a young colored man who carried a knife. The only clue was a loud plaid topcoat which the assailant wore. A young Negro in such a coat was picked up, and identified by two of the three women. After Coakley had been working on the case for some time he became convinced that there was something wrong. The suspect told him that he had had a roommate who was his size and looked very much like him, and who had borrowed his topcoat on numerous occasions. Coakley says:

"Feeling uneasy about the matter, I went to Mr. Warren and told him that I somehow couldn't bring this man into court, where a conviction and a life sentence were certain, when my instinct told me that he might not be guilty. Mr. Warren would never let us go against our instincts; he told me to get the case out of court, and continue the investigation. Then the same crime was

committed by a young Negro in Seattle, also at the point
of a knife, and the assailant apprehended. The Seattle
prisoner confessed that he had committed the three crimes
in Oakland, while wearing his roommate's topcoat. Thus
we had saved a human life and in addition prevented a
tragic miscarriage of justice."

Once Coakley was already in the middle of a murder
trial when he came to the conclusion that the man should
not be convicted. The defendant had been sitting on a
stool in a small restaurant when he had been molested by
a drunk, and knocked to the floor. Infuriated, he had
followed his tormenter into the street and punched him
hard. The drunk had struck his head on the pavement
and died. "The man had a perfectly clear record," says
Coakley, "and before going to the jury with my final
summary I told Mr. Warren how I felt about this. He
replied:

" 'You're down there on the firing line, Frank, and if
that's the way you feel about it, you tell the jury that
you wouldn't convict if you were in their place.' I told
this to the jury and they acquitted the man very fast."

In a third case a big car driving at high speed smashed
into a lighter car at an intersection, killing a father and
son. In the big car were the owner, Schuman, and a
friend by the name of Borelli. Borelli, who was sober,
managed to crawl out of the wreck, but Schuman, who
was drunk, lay sprawled half across the front seat and
the steering wheel. Borelli said that Schuman had been
driving. Schuman said he was too drunk to know
whether he had been driving or not. "We indicted Schuman, but in the middle of the case the defense sprang
two witnesses who maintained that they had seen the car

coming down the street just prior to the accident, and that the man who was driving wore a blue suit. Schuman didn't own a blue suit, and Borelli was wearing a blue suit at the time of the accident. I cross-examined the defense witnesses at length, but couldn't break them down. Their testimony seemed honest and disinterested. I went up to Warren's office and told the District Attorney that I now had the feeling that Schuman was innocent. Warren replied:

" 'Very well, move to dismiss.'

"When I went back to the courtroom I asked the judge to dismiss the defendant, and when this had been done I turned to the bailiff and, pointing to Borelli, said, 'Arrest that man!' Borelli then confessed that he had been driving the car, and had laid the blame on his friend in order to escape the penalties."

Warren went into court himself to secure the convictions of two men who had robbed banks in Berkeley and Oakland. He prosecuted for grand larceny a number of leading stockbrokers and attorneys who had misappropriated estates left in their management. On a second level of operation he did some of his more important work. Alameda County was a haven for swindlers and bunko men who were mulcting the public of millions of dollars every year. The rackets worked in various ways; the so-called Cox Chemical Company sold stock in a "miraculous" process whereby a substance distilled from shale, when dropped into a drum of crude oil, would allegedly increase the yield of gasoline by fifty percent and eliminate all need of cracking. They nicked judges, court clerks and prominent businessmen for as much as ten

thousand dollars each. By the time Warren had collected
enough evidence to bring the officials into court they had
swindled the community out of nearly half a million.
Using the device of getting the company's officials each
into a separate deputy's room, without giving them an
opportunity to prepare their stories in advance, and by
showing each of them the thick folio proving their guilt,
Warren and his deputies succeeded in getting the swindlers to break down and make confessions which convicted them.

The Lusitania Building and Loan Association, which
took money from people without investing it in anything
except the pleasure of its officers, drained the large Por-
tuguese colony almost dry before Warren convicted the
three ringleaders. The Golette Oil Company took money
(four hundred thousand dollars) from the citizens until
Warren secured the conviction of more than twenty involved in the swindle.

But the racket which roused his deepest anger was that
of the health insurance companies whose salesmen covered
the county, extracting thirty-six-dollar policy premiums
from the very poorest people, some of them terribly ill,
promising in return complete medical and hospital insurance, and maintaining no reserve whatever with which
to pay the claims. If the victim did not have thirty-six
dollars in the world, the salesman would take furniture,
clothing, even the few chickens in the yard. Warren
had never forgotten the story of how Methias' brother
had died in Chicago because of lack of money for doctors
or hospitalization, he was already formulating an early
concept for a prepaid health insurance plan; the speed
and strength with which he rounded up the health insur-

ance ring and sent them to San Quentin must have seemed
to these racketeers something akin to the wrath of God.
Word got about that Alameda County had become an
unhealthy place for swindlers.

On the third level, of crimes against the state, he secured
the conviction of a member of the Berkeley Board of
Education who had embezzled thirty thousand dollars of
the school funds; brought about the resignation of the
director of the county's new three-million-dollar psychiatric Highland Hospital, in which the patients were sold
narcotics and literally beaten to death by sadistic employees. He cleaned out of the county jail the men who were
selling narcotics to the prisoners, and secured convictions
of a number of sheriff's deputies and policemen on charges
of bribery. He made frequent raids on Emeryville,
known as the dump heap of the county, where were collected the county's underworld, crooked gambling houses,
bootleggers' dives, dope peddlers' headquarters, red-light
districts; tangling head-on with Sheriff Becker who protected the district, and who got the offenders out of the
county jail and set up in business again. Becker was
clever and Warren still could not get enough evidence
against him to secure a grand jury indictment.

When complaints were registered in the district attorney's office against parents who did not send their children
to school, Warren's investigators generally found the families bogged down in poverty, without shoes or respect-
able clothing for the children to wear to class. Instead
of prosecuting such parents, he and his deputies scoured
the town to get shoes, clothing, food and money for the
destitute family. After he had seen a number of these

cases he decided to take a close look at the Alameda County Charities Commission.

He found their work in complete chaos: people who had sums of money and good jobs were drawing relief, while those in desperate need didn't know where to go for help. The commission itself had no method of determining whether those who applied should be given help. This kind of reorganizational job was meat and drink to Earl Warren, and soon the commission was functioning on a solid base. Much waste was eliminated and greater funds made available for those who hadn't been able to send their children to school.

On the fourth plane, that of remedial work, Warren now evolved his technique of close cooperation of all people involved in doing a governmental job, an organizational plan which he was to extend so effectively as he went on to higher office, and which has remained one of the strongest bases of his success as a public servant. He divided Alameda County into five zones, and in each zone brought together the police chiefs, deputies and other law-enforcement officers. In these meetings the men would discuss their common problems, exchange information on where they had succeeded and where they had failed, and extend their files not only on criminal identification but on criminal methods. He then brought together all the key men in the zones so that they could become acquainted with each other's personalities and activities, and learn to work together in the simplification of each other's tasks. Only Sheriff Becker and the police officers of Emeryville did not participate.

He ran a school in conjunction with his office, calling

in experts to train his investigators and deputies not only
in the taking of evidence, and how to outsmart offenders
and bring in the suspects peaceably by using their wits
rather than their hands, but also in protecting the rights
of the men who were being arrested. Very occasionally,
in a bootlegging arrest, or as in the closing of Little Tia-
juana, there was a fist fight, but in all of the years that
he held office no one of Warren's agents was seriously injured, and more remarkable, no one who was arrested was
badly hurt.

Warren's long-time chief investigator, Oscar Jahnsen,
quotes Warren as saying, "Be fair to everyone, even if
they are breaking the law. Intelligence and proper handling can get confessions quicker than force. Never bluff
on any case. If they call your bluff, you're lost. Get the
facts and then proceed, but get the facts honestly, and
do not color them. If they are there, you will get them;
if not, you don't want them."

He studied the means by which trials were slowed down
to such an extent that public interest vanished and the
culprit got off; then he wrote new laws to speed up the
process, laws which he presented to the board of supervisors, as well as to the state legislature. He took an
important part in the work of the State Association of
District Attorneys, compiling a code of uniform methods, serving as the association's president, and then for
many years as its executive secretary. In this capacity
his task was to write the needed laws, then go up to
Sacramento and guide them through the legislature. He
started a course at the University of California, the first
of its kind in America, where methods of trial procedure
were studied, and new formulas evolved.

He had become a scientist in the eradication of crime and the modernizing of legal procedure. If these had been his only virtues little more would have been heard of him, but woven through all his actions and all of his work was a "fourth dimension" of sensitivity, of love for people, compassion for those in trouble, and indestructible sense of fair play.

VII. Government Is a Science

In 1930 Warren came up for re-election, and won by the largest majority in Alameda County history. Just before the primary Sheriff Becker had finally crawled far out on a limb, and there stood Warren waiting, ready to saw it off behind him.

A group of paving contractors in Oakland banded together and through collusion with members of the city council obtained a monopoly on paving contracts. Not only did this eliminate competitive bidding, but it defrauded the city out of millions of dollars by furnishing a poor grade of paving, and fulfilling the majority of its contracts on paper rather than on the streets. In addition they forced all independent paving companies out of business, and when a small home owner wished to have a piece of sidewalk put in front of his house, it would cost him three hundred dollars for a fifty-dollar job. The kickbacks on the colossal graft were paid to the city commissioner who awarded the contracts, to other city officials, and to Sheriff Becker. What made the case delicate to handle was that the contractors

were now millionaires, and represented some of the oldest and most influential families in the community.

It was not enough for District Attorney Warren to
subpoena the records and awards of the city council to
the Greater Oakland Construction Company. Neither
was it adequate to subpoena the books of the paving
companies and determine how much money they had
spent, and how much work they actually had done.
Nor would it be sufficient to have the testimony only of
small home owners who had been robbed, or districts
that had been forced to pay assessments for which they
had received little or no benefits. All of this might
come under the heading of bad or stupid city management. What he needed was the testimony of city officials who had been paid off, persons who had acted as
go-betweens, men who could bring proof into court of
the corruption and conspiracy between the Oakland
officials and the construction company.

He offered immunity to the lower-paid Oakland officials who might now be willing to make their bed on
the side of the law; the paving ring and its henchmen
in the government were so powerful that no city employee dared accept. Stymied at every turn, Warren
took his records and books before the grand jury, asking
for the indictment of Commissioner of Public Works
Parker, of Sheriff Becker, of contractor Harry Lesser.
Feeling that he could not break the combine without
public support and that he had no way of getting this
support unless he could make known the grand jury
testimony, Warren released each day's proceedings to
the reporters. The accused maintained that Warren
acted illegally; Warren quoted the California statute

which says, ". . . members of the Grand Jury may not disclose evidence," but does not prohibit the district attorney from doing so.

When the public saw the extent to which it was being victimized, and the brazenness with which it was being bilked, it turned against the elected officers and influential families and backed the District Attorney solidly in his demand that the grafters be brought to trial.

"The public never turned me down. I took my story right to them, told them the facts bluntly, and when we got into a pinch they stayed with us." Now, with the pressure of public opinion behind him, Warren was able to persuade policemen, sheriff's deputies and assistants in the commissioner's office to bring him their proofs of the passage of money from the Greater Oakland Construction Company to the public officials. Caught red-handed, Sheriff Becker resigned. But Warren promptly filed his case in the Oakland courts.

Becker went about brandishing his revolver and exclaiming to anyone who would listen:

"Why should I worry? See this gun, it's got two bullets in it, one for me and the other for Warren—if he don't lay off me!"

Rough voices telephoned to the Warren home, saying, "Mrs. Warren? You tell your husband to lay off this prosecution or your children will never get home from school."

As far as Becker's threat was concerned, Warren believed that barking dogs don't bite. But he and Nina Warren did have a serious discussion over the threat to their two sons and daughter, wondering if they should give the children police protection, or send them away for a few weeks so they would be safe. In the end they decided that either of these alternatives would have an injurious effect upon the youngsters, and that all the Warrens had better just go on about their normal lives.

"I never brought the subject of crime or criminals into my home," says Governor Warren. "I hated crime, and the whole unhappy, sordid business of arrests, convictions, prisons. Youngsters are terribly impressionable, and I didn't want their lives blighted or malformed from exposure to my work. That's why I didn't allow officials or lawyers to come to my home in the evening. If the matter were of sufficient importance they could telephone me at any hour, and I would get up, dress and go down to my office."

Warren knew that the public grows fatigued if the big graft cases are too long and drawn out. The men under indictment knew this too and used every device, legal and otherwise, to get the cases postponed until the public would become bored with the whole affair, for then they had a good chance of beating the rap. But Warren never allowed the cases to drag or grow cold; he pushed hard, working night and day, preparing his briefs, and staying in the courts and with the judges to secure immediate trials.

The lawyers for the pavers tried delaying tactics half a dozen times, but Warren was always there in the courtroom to pose the public's legal rights against those of the ring's, and the opposing attorneys never secured any of their greatly desired postponements.

Pavers and public officials alike were convicted and sent to San Quentin.

Within the next weeks, when Warren warned the

Commissioner of Public Health and Safety to resign, the men responsible for the city's smelly garbage deal cleaned their houses and garbage pails mighty fast. With Sheriff Becker no longer able to protect them, the last of the gambling halls and speakeasies in Emeryville were permanently closed down. Warren then went to bat for higher wages for policemen and deputies so that these men could support their families on their salaries, and thus be removed from the temptations of bribery.

When a new district attorney was elected in San Francisco, he announced in his acceptance speech, "I am going to overhaul this department and pattern it on the work and methods of Earl Warren." Raymond Moley, after a national survey, called Earl Warren's the best-run district attorney's office in the country.

By this time Earl Warren decided that he too ought to have a raise. He had been receiving six thousand dollars a year for handling the third largest district attorney's office in the state, a job which in San Francisco and Los Angeles was divided between the district attorney and city attorney, costing those counties eighteen thousand dollars and twenty thousand dollars a year. He asked for his wage to be raised to nine thousand dollars. The board of supervisors compromised at seven thousand, two hundred.

He had need of the extra salary, for his family was growing apace. Virginia, his first daughter, was born on September 13, 1928, and Earl Jr. was born on January 31, 1930. The family now bought their first home on quiet, residential Larkspur Road in Oakland, with a lawn in front and a flower garden behind. A second daughter, Dorothy, was born on June 12, 1931, and the carpenters were busy adding another bedroom. When each child was three months old, Earl asked Nina to bring the baby to the office for a little party, with each of the deputies holding the infant in turn. These impromptu affairs, and the annual Christmas dinner at the Sequoia Club for the entire office, at which "joke-presents" were exchanged, such as a large alarm clock for the deputy who always rushed in a minute or two late, were the only social events during the year in which he mixed his private and professional life.

The Warrens indulged in little outside social activity. Nina Warren, who took care of her home and four children, would have had little opportunity for it; Earl Warren, who still maintained a hard schedule, had small chance to build an active social life, with its mounting round of dinner parties, card games and dances. He was away from home often, traveling the state on business and to attend meetings, which would have disrupted any attempt at an organized social calendar. There were frequent official visits to Oakland of representatives of the federal government, as well as district attorneys from other counties. These guests he would take to the club for dinner.

He had given up his Sunday golf on the day Virginia was born, saying, "If I don't spend my one free day with my children, when will I ever get acquainted with them?"

After church he would fit his blond-haired, blue-eyed, healthy, open-faced youngsters into canvas seats in the car, and drive to Lake Merritt to feed the ducks, eat popcorn and ice cream and romp on the rolling

green lawns, enjoying his own relaxation in the out-
doors, while Mrs. Warren had her one completely quiet,
restful period at home, also recouping her energies.
Thus the Warrens were a world unto themselves, utterly
happy inside the love and confidence of their own fast-
growing family circle.

With his office running smoothly and efficiently, and
ninety percent of the backlog of crime obliterated,
Warren had an opportunity to devote more of his time
to a subject which had always fascinated him. He
planned the reorganization of the county structure, and
set up a modern and highly workable charter for
Alameda County which brought the residents a far
greater share of local self-government. He helped or-
ganize the Legal Aid Society, became president of the
Board of Managers of the State Bureau of Criminal
Identification, and worked with this bureau for the immediate communication of information on criminals.
He wrote an ordinance creating a Department of Charities for the more effective use of the county's funds,
asked for relief bonds to prevent suffering in the depres-
sion, and when the Volstead Act was repealed, submitted a bill calling for restricted licensing, with thorough character investigation, so that the gangsters
might be kept out.

As district attorney he had come into frequent contact with the attorney general's office, and here he saw
things which distressed him as greatly as had the organization inside the district attorney's office many
years before. There was no central agency or head of
law enforcement in the state, the hundreds of district

attorneys, sheriffs and police chiefs working in lonely, local isolation. There was little cooperation between the various geographic sections, and no advisor to whom they could turn for counsel, aid or support. Warren had long since come to the conclusion that the logical head of this work should be the state's attorney general.

The then attorney general was Ulysses S. Webb, who had been in office for thirty-one consecutive years and was seventy-one years of age. It was said in California, "No use running against U. S. Webb; people think that when they are voting for him they are voting for the federal government."

Webb received only five thousand dollars a year as salary, and was obliged to devote much of his time to private practice. His deputies were paid only two hundred dollars a month, taking the job for the prestige, free desk space and secretarial services for their outside practice.

"In those days the attorney general's calendar was half as thick as a Bible," says Warren, "and the litigation ran years behind. When state officers asked for an opinion from the attorney general, the request often kicked around the office for months. There was no central record or bookkeeping system, and everybody was on his own. Deputies picked up certain cases, kept the papers in their own desks, and then threw them away when the case was over. No one could ever be held responsible for any case or opinion. I had a pretty tightly run organization in the district attorney's office, and I thought that the important law work of the state called for tighter organization."

It was only natural that a man as physically and mentally vigorous as Earl Warren should now be looking for a tougher and more important assignment. Here was a new challenge, and a job that sorely needed doing.

It is probable that by campaigning vigorously and exposing the disorder inside the attorney general's office, he could have defeated Webb. Instead he went to the Attorney General and said, "Mr. Webb, I want to tell you that when you are ready to leave this office, I am going to file for the position. However, I also want you to know that I will never file against you, or make any effort whatever to take your job away as long as you want it."

Meanwhile he studied the state constitution and perceived that in order to make the attorney general's office a really creative force within the state, the constitution would have to be revised. He wrote a series of constitutional amendments which changed the nature of the office, and made it the second most important and effective within the state government. Backed solidly by the District Attorneys Association, he worked with civic organizations until a constitutional amendment raised the attorney general's salary from five thousand dollars a year to eleven thousand dollars a year, but at the same time prohibited him from carrying on any private practice.

The newspapers and politicians around San Francisco Bay smiled and said, "Earl Warren is making a good job for himself." This was of course true, though Webb was making considerably more than eleven thousand a year by his combination of attorney general's salary plus private practice.

It was to be five long years before Attorney General

Webb would finally retire at the age of seventy-six. All this time Warren stood in grave danger of having him die in office, which would mean that the Governor would appoint one of his own political cronies, and in an election, the incumbent always has the edge. It was a gamble in human decency, one which Earl Warren was fully willing to take.

By the time the election of 1934 rolled around, Earl Warren's proposed year and a half in the district attorney's office had stretched to fourteen years. He would have liked to move up to the attorney general's office, but he had given his promise not to disturb Webb, and there was no further thought of going back into private practice.

"You have to have a baptism of fire in the public service," said Warren, "then you either fold, or are committed for life. I knew I was spoiled for private practice because of the satisfaction I had had from public service."

However, his third term as district attorney was to prove no less exciting than the last: for the first time in its history the office found itself before the grand jury with three major cases, the indictment of the entire city government of Alameda, the board of equalization scandal, and the *Point Lobos* ship murder.

Warren's deputies often said, "He had an instinct about things that were going wrong. He knew about them almost before they happened." When a member of the City Council of Alameda resigned, Warren commented, "Something strange is going on over there. Let's look into it."

His instinct proved right: investigation showed that the City Manager, who had been hired to take care of the business of the town, had involved the Mayor and all but one of the city councilmen in a graft setup which had not only been pilfering the city's funds, but had organized protection rackets which were bleeding the local merchants dry.

Summoned before the grand jury, they held out with a great deal of bravado until they were faced with some of their own signed receipts; then one of the key men broke and exposed the entire sordid story. The Mayor and councilmen pleaded guilty and were sent to the county jail for short terms. The City Manager was sent to San Quentin.

The board of equalization scandal involved the chief liquor-enforcement officer of the board and his assistant, who were indicted for accepting bribes from illegal liquor dealers. A judge in the city of Albany was charged with soliciting a bribe on the grounds that he, the judge, could fix things up with the board of equalization . . . for a certain sum of money. The chief law-enforcement officer went to San Quentin and the judge went to the county jail, losing both his judgeship and his right to practice law.

The S. S. *Point Lobos* murder was the most tumultuous case in his career as district attorney. The ship's chief engineer, George Alberts, was murdered in his cabin while his ship was tied to the dock in Alameda, his skull bashed in by a bludgeon and one leg almost severed from his body by the hacking of a big knife. Alberts was a good citizen, thirty-seven years old, with a wife and three children; his only offense was that he had had a dispute with one of the members of the crew over wages at the end of the voyage. He had also been outspoken in his opposition to the American Communists. Though there was always considerable tension between the maritime unions and the ship owners, at the particular moment when George Alberts was murdered there was no actual conflict.

It appeared that Frank Conner, who was the union delegate on the *Point Lobos*, had complained to Earl King, secretary of the Marine Firemen, Oilers, Water Tenders and Wipers Union, that Alberts had discharged a union member of the engine-room crew without paying all the overtime money due, and asked that a union patrol be sent over to the *Point Lobos* "to get the matter fixed up." King, Conner and E. G. Ramsay, also a union official, sent George Wallace and Ben Sakowitz to beat up Chief Engineer Alberts, giving them thirty dollars of union funds for the "expedition across the Bay." Former Attorney General Robert W. Kenny of California, who has long been sympathetic to the C.I.O., says today, "The union officials told Sakowitz to beat the engineer within an inch of his life, but he forgot to take a ruler."

The truth as Warren determined it was somewhat more subtle: the union officials were content to have Alberts beaten up, for their grievance was an economic one. Sakowitz had a political motive: he killed the engineer in order to get an active anti-Communist out of the way. Warren was shocked at the brutal slaying as he never had been shocked before; there flashed into his mind that very earliest image, when he had been only four years old, of the man who had been hanged in effigy in the yard of the Ann Street School.

Harry Bridges and the maritime unions of San Francisco exerted the heaviest possible pressure to keep him from investigating the murder, threatening political reprisals if he attacked the union involved, but Warren was grimly determined to bring in the men responsible. For six months his office worked night and day to build a chain of evidence. They said little to the public until they were ready, then arrested King, Ramsay, Conner and Wallace for the conspiracy to murder Chief Engineer Alberts. Sakowitz was never found.

The furor which the Maritime Union set up was like nothing ever seen or heard on the Pacific Coast before. The arrested men were called martyrs in the cause of labor, while Warren was labeled a reactionary, an enemy of organized labor whose sole purpose in arresting these persons was to smash the unions. Every day during the trial Harry Bridges sent literally thousands of pickets to march solidly in a mass line around the courthouse, carrying banners which extolled the virtues of King, Ramsay, Conner and Wallace, and vilified Earl Warren. Massed pickets also surrounded the Warren home in an effort to intimidate the family. Yet while the radical press of San Francisco was filling the air with its poison-pen diatribes, Wallace confessed to having acted as a guard while Sakowitz murdered the engineer, and Conner confessed that he, King and Ramsay had sent Wallace and Sakowitz to "tamp-up" the engineer for his anti-union activities. King never denied his guilt.

Since it was no longer possible to declare the accused men innocent, the tactic shifted to prove Earl Warren guilty. He was accused of assigning the case to one judge and then, without explanation, transferring it to the court of another judge who had been appointed to the bench on Warren's recommendation. He was accused of being aware that one of his deputies was borrowing large sums of money from one of the jurors. He was accused of having the jury panels supplied by "various industrial plants, business houses, the Bank of America, the American Trust Company." He was accused of letting important prosecution witnesses accept a regular monthly remittance from the shipping firm which owned the *Point Lobos*.

Since the four men had not committed the actual murder, Warren asked for a second-degree verdict, rather than the death sentence. Former Governor Olson, whose parole board released Ramsey, King and Conner after they had served little over four years, says today, "I read the entire transcript of evidence when I first refused these men a pardon, and there was no doubt but that they had sent Wallace and Sakowitz to beat up the engineer. Nor is there any doubt that they had a fair trial."

The extreme left-wing clique of the C.I.O. would never forgive Warren for this case; they still fill the air with their furious charges. However, Earl Warren has continued to carry every A.F.L. and C.I.O. stronghold in the state, proving that the rank and file of labor care no more for brutal political murders than had the District Attorney himself. Joseph R. Knowland, editor and publisher of the Oakland *Tribune* says:

No one ever told Warren what to do in the line of duty, at least not more than once. I lost several friends who asked me to intervene in some important matter with Warren, and wouldn't believe me when I told them

I couldn't influence Warren, and that if I tried to interfere it would only hurt them or their friends. He never
tried to control politics in town; all he wanted was the
best possible government. The only people who tried to
attack him were those whom he had attacked for good
and valid reasons. Our paper backed him all the way
through, and so did all the other papers. He sought
advice from his friends on every legitimate subject, but
when he had a job to perform he went ahead on his own
responsibility.

In the early spring of 1938, when U. S. Webb was
seventy-six, he finally went to Warren, thanked him for
his patience and consideration, and said that he was not
going to run for attorney general again.

Earl Warren immediately announced his candidacy,
had petitions signed by Republican, Democratic and
Progressive voters, then posted the required two-
hundred-dollar filing fee for candidacy in each of the
three parties.

VIII. Nonpartisanship Is an Art

THE CALIFORNIA election laws are very nearly inexplicable to anyone who has not drunk them in with his mother's milk; and even after an outsider has understood them from the viewpoint of politics, he still goes through life failing to understand them on the basis of logic. The entire enigma is contained in the phrase *crossfiling:* under this system a man whose family has been Republican ever since Fremont's campaign in 1856, and who will not even play handball with a Democrat, not only enters his name in the Republican primary but also files his name on the Democratic ticket, dreaming that a majority of the Democrats of the state will vote for him, as well as a majority of the Republicans, and thus he will be elected in the June primary and be spared the need to spend the next four months touring the state and making a thousand speeches. By the same token a lifetime Democrat, even one who still thinks of the Republicans as carpetbaggers, will file on the Republican ticket in California as well as the Democratic and hope that enough Republicans will give him a majority of their votes in the primary to save him the time, energy and cost of campaigning. No Californian has ever been able to say why Democrats vote for Republicans, or vice versa, but they continue to do so in large numbers. The only explanation proffered for the confusing state of affairs is that it tends to soften party lines and party animosity, to make the people of the state, as far as politics is concerned, one big happy family.

The district attorney's office was nonpartisan; neither Warren nor any other aspirant to that post ever had been obliged to put down his party affiliation on the ballot. The campaign for attorney general in 1938 would be Earl Warren's first party election. Despite the fact that he was an announced Republican, he filed on all three tickets—and so did his opponents.

He made a vigorous campaign, but the activity was hardly necessary: he had now been working for some fifteen years in the closest cooperation with every city, town and hamlet in the state, had acted for the welfare of teachers, policemen, firemen and other public officials, and participated in a hundred phases of the state's activities, all the way from instructing at the University of California to rewriting parts of the state's constitution. When the full primary vote was counted, California enjoyed a new political experience: Warren actually had been elected attorney general not only by the Republicans but by the Democrats and Progressives as well.

He was one of the few Republicans to survive the Democratic landslide of 1938, which had resulted from the growth of the Democratic party in California under the national leadership of Franklin D. Roosevelt. Culbert L. Olson, a former Utah lawyer, became California's first Democratic governor since the turn of the century, a circumstance which was to cause one of the most dramatic internecine wars the state ever had known and propel an unwilling Earl Warren into a foremost position on the national scene.

"I decided to behave like a new broom on my first day as attorney general," relates Warren, "and got to the office at nine o'clock sharp."

Arriving there he found two telephone messages, one of which informed him that the retiring Republican Governor Merriam's personal secretary had been selling pardons to San Quentin and Folsom prisoners on a cash basis, the second telling him that this devious gentleman had been appointed to the California bench by Merriam only the night before. By nine-fifteen Warren had the miscreant in his office, and was taking the deposition which not only kept the man from becoming a judge, but led to his subsequent conviction.

Warren had promised a nonpartisan regime, but this instantaneous fulfillment left the state gasping. One editor chuckled, "It is now going to be difficult to distinguish between Republican misdemeanors and Democratic torts," while another newspaper said in astonishment, "We knew the fur would fly when Warren took office, but we never expected it to be Republican fur." Manchester Boddy, publisher of the only Democratic, prolabor newspaper in Southern California, the *Daily News*, commented, "I believe that official California is in for a good scrubbing behind the ears."

Having eliminated this sale-of-pardons blight, Warren suggested an idea on which he had been working. Whereas a pardoned man recovers all of his rights of citizenship and freedom of activity, the paroled prisoner recovers none of these rights, must report to the parole board constantly, is limited in his travel and associations, and bears a stigma which often affects his employment. The legal process of securing a pardon was expensive and was available only to those who had political influence. Warren suggested a "simple device whereby any man, having discharged his debt to society, might rehabilitate himself by registering with the county clerk that he intends to seek a pardon, and for a set period of time reporting to the local police chief, to the sheriff and to the district attorney. He could then go into court and petition for restoration of citizenship, and the state's officials could testify for him. I would like to have it made a penal offense for any lawyer, any public official or any other man to take a five-cent piece from a former convict thus earning back his citizenship."

The attorney general's office was located in San Francisco and occupied the sixth floor of the white stone State Building facing the Civic Center. Warren had a big oak-paneled room, with corner windows and pigeons from the City Hall Park nesting on the cornices. *The California Codes and General Laws* in their red bindings sat on the desk immediately within reach of his hand. The room was well lighted, with a full-length gray carpet.

As he had long ago planned one of his early corrective acts as attorney general was to arrange for the raising of the deputies' wages to six and seven hundred dollars a month, prohibiting them from practicing on the outside. At this salary he could get excellent men who would devote their entire attention to their job. He gradually weeded out any misfits in the office and gathered round him fifty young and energetic lawyers. He departmentalized the work into divisions of taxes, litigation, collections, criminal work and opinions for the state. The deputies who were most interested and talented in these divisions were made specialists in their fields. Thousands of antiquated cases were disposed of and the calendar brought up to date.

He persuaded William T. Sweigert, one of the state's ablest lawyers, and a lifetime Democrat, to take charge of the reorganization of the handling of the enormous calendar of civil court cases. "This is a law office for the people of California," he told Sweigert, "and I want to make it the best law office in the state. Study the methods used in our biggest and best private firms, and bring back to us everything valuable you can learn."

While Sweigert was making his survey, Warren extended his idea of securing close cooperation of all the individual groups within the state. And as he had done with Alameda County, the state was now divided into zones, and every other month he met with the district attorney and other law-enforcement heads of each zone. Every office had a different kind of problem, and these were thrown into the common discussion, with everyone helping to find a solution. After a time this tightly knit working together gave the agencies confidence in each other, and in the attorney general's office. They knew that no matter how complex or harassed or dangerous their assignments, they would have the full and immediate support of the attorney general's office, and all of its resources. Thus Warren's office came to serve as a clearing house of experience and knowledge for all the zones and all the communities.

"Very soon we had friendly relations, and were getting close cooperation," says Warren. "If the district attorney in any city or county found that he was not strong enough to cope with the local criminals, racketeers, swindlers, or crooked politicians, he knew that he could call upon the attorney general's office, and every other district attorney within the state. We gave each other confidence, a sense of security, and the genuine conviction that the state could be kept clean of criminal conspiracies. Men working together in this close fashion are always likely to do a better job."

One observer said, "Warren has 'chummed-up' the law-enforcement officers of the state."

When Sweigert completed his survey, Warren and he converted the attorney general's office into a completely modern, streamlined organization. The three offices in San Francisco, Sacramento and Los Angeles were coordinated, with central filing and information systems.

"We knew who was handling everything," says Warren, "and kept each matter moving along. Every deputy attorney general reported very quickly after getting his assignment, and kept progress reports not only filled out, but very much in evidence. After awhile we knew exactly how long every type of case should take; when state officials asked for opinions we got them out in written form in a matter of days, and we were ready to back our opinions with sound reasoning and documentation."

While he had been district attorney none of the illegal dog tracks had dared to open in his bailiwick, but they had surrounded his county.

"When I came into office there were seven tracks holding dog races. There was no supervision over these tracks; the odds were fixed, and so were the dogs. It was just a plain racket and I made up my mind that this open violation must stop. Every track had its own season, so they did not conflict with each other, and the track which happened to be open at the time was El Cerrito, run by Black Jack Jerome, a former San Francisco strikebreaker. Our office worked up the whole case, and when we were ready to go into court, I asked Jerome to come to see me. He asked if he might bring his lawyer. I said yes, and when they arrived I told them, 'I don't want to put you out of business the hard way, but you're breaking the law, and you'll have to go.' Jerome asked, 'Are you going to treat all the tracks the same, or are you just picking on us?' When I replied that all tracks would be treated the same, Black Jack asked permission to confer with his lawyer in the outside hall. When they returned a few moments later, he said, 'This is Wednesday. Can we operate through Saturday night, and then close?' "

Warren replied with a faint smile, "I cannot give you permission to continue an illegal activity, but I hardly think this office would be prepared to issue an order until Monday morning, and so if you shut down Saturday night, we would have no reason to issue that complaint."

Black Jack was the toughest operator in the state. When he closed down peaceably none of the other tracks even attempted to open. Thus the state avoided a number of suits, and an outward display of force, which Warren so heartily disliked. It was ever his hope to get people to see that they were breaking the law, and that his office had prepared the case so thoroughly that they would be found guilty in the courts. To the operators who maintained that the public enjoyed this form of entertainment, Warren replied, "If you don't like what I am doing, change the law. While that is the law, it must be enforced." Never a year passes but that the gamblers try to change the law.

For many years he had watched the national syndicates drain millions of dollars from California residents, but he had been powerless to act. When Warren assumed the office of attorney general he commented, ". . . no one is running a big gambling establishment without paying off public officials."

He hauled the bookmakers and wire services into court, securing convictions every time. The newspapers began to talk about the "Warren Crusade," and occasionally he was called a reformer. He countered with, "As a law-enforcement officer I have no right to question the wisdom of these statutes, or to temporize in enforcing them." Actually he disapproved of organized gambling, for he had watched the pennies of the reliefers and the dollars of the employed roll into the bottomless pocket of the professional gambler, too often causing suffering among the victimized wives and children.

The case that attracted the widest national attention was that of Tony Cornero, a millionaire gambler who had opened a luxury ship called the *Rex,* off Long Beach, beyond the three-mile limit. Some of the games were fixed; with others the house took such a large percentage that the player had to lose.   There were fights, beatings and a complete lack of supervision over the water-taxis which carried the suckers out to the *Rex*. There was a general impression that the people of California were powerless to control Cornero because he was operating in international waters; Warren thought otherwise.

"No criminal can stay in business against the law-enforcement officer who knows his business, and is determined to close him up."

The attorney general's office spent several months preparing its case, then Warren sent Oscar Jahnsen out to see Cornero.   Oscar went aboard, told Tony that the Attorney General had sent him a warning that he was operating illegally, and must shut down.   Tony laughed good-naturedly.

"Ah, I'm out in the clear.   There's nothing anybody can do about me.   Come on, Oscar, let me show you this terrific plant I have here."   He then showed Oscar over the ship, while Warren's chief investigator took copious notes on what he saw.

Warren next went down to Long Beach and put together a fleet of State Fish and Game Commission cutters, fire ships and fishing vessels manned by law-enforcement officers who boarded the *Rex*, destroyed the gambling equipment, and ended the ship's career. No one was hurt in the operation.

Most Californians thought that now Cornero would sue for damages.   Instead Cornero's lawyer agreed to pay the state's complete cost of the case, some fifteen thousand dollars.

On a higher level of creative government Warren began an investigation of the private and public asylums about which he had numerous complaints, and of the seven thousand private homes in which orphaned children were under the care of private families; helped end discrimination against Negro boxers at the Hollywood Legion Stadium; ruled that policemen and state troopers could not have undercover license plates, but had to operate out in the open; made it possible for the state's elder citizens to retain what little property they might have, in particular their homes, and still draw their modest pensions. He withstood the pressure of California's exporters who threatened to move to another state, declaring that the state's sales tax must apply to all merchandise sold for shipment abroad, thus earning the state some three million dollars of income a year. He issued an injunction against the Montebello Oil Company which was using illegal drilling methods to increase its oil output at the expense of some $3,500,000 wastage of natural gas. He represented the State of California before the United States Supreme Court on twelve separate occasions, and spent most of March, 1939, in Washington, testifying before Congress on the question of California's oil-bearing tidelands, submitting briefs for the state's continued ownership. He rendered opinions in local and interstate boundary disputes, handled many phases of the two-hundred-million-dollar liquidation of the Pacific Mutual Insurance Company, and the solvency proceedings of the fifty-million-dollar Pacific States Building and Loan Association. He and his deputies brought three thousand civil cases to completion, and at no time did his office have fewer than two thousand separate cases, large and small, pending before the courts. In addition the office wrote three thousand opinions for state officials, boards, commissions and legislators.

As a fitting climax to his four-year term, when California's Accounting Department added up the amount of money the state had recovered through the attorney general's suits and negotiations on tax cases, as well as contracts, the total amounted to more than the attorney general's entire office had cost the tax-payers.

In the meanwhile Earl and Nina Warren's family had literally burst out of their Larkspur Road house, for they now had the six children they had agreed would make an ideal family. Their third daughter, Nina, had been born on October 15, 1933, and their third son, Robert, on January 9, 1935. They found a big, old rambling house with seven bedrooms and a third floor study for Earl, at 88 Vernon Street, in Oakland, just a block above the Piedmont Baths where they had first met in 1921. Here the six children grew apace, their toys, tricycles and bicycles strewn about a big back yard with its flower beds and fruit trees. Jim, the oldest boy, nicknamed the youngsters as they came along: Virginia managed to escape, but Earl Jr. became Ju-Ju, Dorothy was foreshortened to Dotty, Nina acquired the title of Honey Bear, and Robert was of course known from the very beginning as Bobby.

Warren believed in local autonomy not only for cities and counties, but for children as well. The six Warren youngsters grew to be such a close clan that when their father would take one of them down to Bakersfield to visit their grandparents, the rest of them would be literally sick with longing until the missing one returned home. In spite of this cohesiveness, all six were distinct and rugged personalities: Jim was the artist in the family, and from his earliest days had clutched his mother's or father's hand as they walked along the streets, saying "Wait for me" while he stood in awe before the colorful advertising on a billboard. He was determined that when he grew up he would be a commercial artist. Virginia was the gay member of the family, excited about her piano and dancing lessons, and the Saturday afternoon parties. Earl Jr. loved everything about outdoor life; he helped his mother raise the flowers which she arranged artistically throughout the house, but his greatest thrill came when his father took him wild-boar hunting on Santa Cruz and Santa Rosa Islands or deep-sea fishing. Bobby had become such a good shot that on one trip with a number of his father's friends he was the only one to bring down a boar. Dotty was the family type, preferring to stay at home with her mother and help bake a big cake for one of the children's birthdays, taking care of Honey Bear, who was two years younger, and Bobby, who was four years younger. In a sense she was her parents' deputy to the other youngsters, arbitrating arguments and helping her father on their Sunday trips to the zoo or picnics back in the Berkeley Hills. Honey Bear and Bobby were a little too young to have manifested their lifetime character as yet, but all six of the children were blond-haired, blue-eyed, open-faced, handsome, husky, happy, a tribute to their mother who, at one period, had representatives in five out of the six grammar-school grades!

Then came the only tragedy that ever befell the Warrens. Earl's mother had left the Bakersfield home for a visit with her daughter in Oakland. While Methias sat reading the newspaper in the living room on a warm summer evening, someone, presumably a prowling tramp, crossed the Warren back yard, saw through the open door that Methias was alone, picked up a rusted piece of pipe which lay half buried in the ground, crept silently into the house and struck the seventy-three-year-old man on the head. Methias managed to stumble as far as his own bed, and there he died. The tramp took Methias' wallet and hurried off, scattering the papers from the billfold on the street as he ran. Itinerants are the most difficult of all criminals to track down; the murder remains unsolved to this day.

Crystal Warren remained with her daughter in Oakland, where Earl and his sister were able to watch over her until her death the following year.

IX. "I Am an Advocate by Nature"

AFTER his discharge from the Army in 1919, Earl Warren had joined the Officers Reserve Corps and served
for fifteen years. His theory about the military was
typically Western: no one ever picks on a man who is
able to defend himself.

Almost two years before Pearl Harbor he went to
Washington, D. C., to participate in the Federal-State
Conference on Law Enforcement Problems of National
Defense, and there he helped to draft recommendations
for all state and local councils. Immediately upon his
return to California he called together his own enforcement heads, and having a strong presentiment that war
might come to the United States, passed on to them the
results of the Washington conference, then divided the
state into nine regions and asked the officers to set up
emergency organizations in their own localities and to
begin preliminary training of their men.

When France fell, Warren called them back for a
conference in conjunction with the Army, Navy,
F.B.I. and the state's fire chiefs, U. S. Foresters, road

and water engineers, communications specialists, radio technicians and highway patrol. His opening greeting contained the essence of Earl Warren's lifetime political philosophy:

> Gentlemen: I want to start our conference by telling you what prompted this gathering. I am sure that all of us realize the possibility of our country being involved in war. But I am not so sure that we fully realize what problems war will bring to us as law-enforcement officers. None of our agencies has been set up to meet war conditions. None of them has the territorial jurisdiction, the personnel or the equipment to do all the things that are necessary to protect, under such circumstances, the community which it serves. No community, regardless of its size, can be self-sufficient in a time of war.
>
> You, of course, appreciate that this entire program is voluntary in character. We have not the right, nor do we desire to superimpose state agencies or state authority over the local law-enforcement agencies. We merely desire to bring them together to work for their common good. We want every community to plan for itself and, in so doing, to lend mutual aid and assistance to its neighbors in times of stress.

In order to give the conference a vivid picture of what modern war actually meant, he introduced a Catholic Sister who had lived for twelve years in France and then walked all the way across France, Spain and Portugal before escaping to America. For five hours the Sister described the chaos that comes when bombs fall on cities, destroying the light, power and water systems; the sabotage of the fifth columnists whose activities go all the way from spreading alarms to blowing up bridges; the strafing and bombing of fleeing civilians in order to clog the roads so that neither troops nor supplies can pass; the kind of air-raid shelters that are needed; the halting of the streams of refugees from destroyed towns; the test of the fire department when a whole city is burning, and of the health department when the streets are piled high with the dead.

This state conference, which was the first of its kind to be held in the country, then proceeded to study every type of emergency problem arising out of war: sabotage, bombing by enemy aircraft, floods, civil riot, pestilence, fire, military invasion, gas attacks, evacuation. In their eleven days of hard discussion the officers tried to anticipate all possible situations, then work out plans to meet them. At the end of the conference they went home to train their own men, and civilian volunteers as well. The results of the conference were published in a book by the California State Department of Education, fifteen hundred copies of which were distributed throughout the country to aid other states.

During the months of spring and summer he continued his defense activities, arranging for F.B.I. schools in each of the nine regions, where some two thousand local police officers were trained in disaster planning and the moving of military equipment and civilian population on highways. The University of California at Berkeley and Los Angeles was used for special study of civilian defense, with the armed forces supplying instructors and the state sending its police, fire, forestry and engineering officers for training. By the end of January, 1941, control centers had been set up in every

county in the state, out of which operated auxiliary firemen, rescue squads, air-raid wardens, nurse's-aide corps,
emergency medical field units, demolition and clearance
squads, and emergency food and housing corps. Just as
important was the expression of the alternate side of
Warren's nature: he set up a Civilian Rights Committee whose purpose it was to train the civilian defense
officers in guarding the rights and liberties of everyone
in the state during any potential emergency.

Because Earl Warren believed that a democracy must
govern itself through laws, and that good laws can always be secured when valid and sufficient reasons are
provided, he next turned to the legislature for help in
preparing for defense. The two acts for which he secured passage were the Uniform Sabotage Prevention
Act, and the Mutual Assistance Act. This latter piece
of legislation was of special importance because for
years there had been a tragic situation in California; if
a house were burning just across the street from the end
of a city or county line, the neighboring fire department were not permitted to cross the street and put out
the fire because they could not collect for any injury to
their person or destruction of their equipment. For a
long time Warren had been working with the city councils, urging them to set up mutual aid pacts whereby
policemen or firemen could cross over into each other's
territories and still be protected. He had secured a good
deal of voluntary cooperation, mostly through his personal influence. Now, with the statewide act passed by
the legislature, mutual aid became a living reality, and
no longer were the citizens of California treated to the

ironic spectacle of a whole fire department standing idle by its trucks, watching property burn down a few yards away.

The Warren Sabotage Act set up defense rings around shipyards, airplane and parts factories. When the labor unions learned of the act their leaders protested that such a defense ring could easily restrain their union activities. Warren assured them that this was not the intent of the act, and that it would not be used for anti-union activities. Labor union officials know that the assurances of state officers are of very little value once a law gets on the statute books, but they also knew that over a period of twenty years as district attorney and attorney general, Earl Warren had never broken a promise to them. They accepted his word, the act was passed, but very promptly a judge of the Los Angeles Circuit Court issued an injunction to prohibit picketing at a factory where a union was in a dispute with management.

Warren dashed down to Los Angeles, went into conference with the judge, explained that such a restraining order was a violation of the intent of the law; he then indicated the legal base on which he, the attorney general, would fight the injunction. It was promptly withdrawn.

This did not stop other factories from trying to use the sabotage law against their workmen. Each time Warren explained, "This law was pointed against the crippling of national-defense industries by spies and traitors, and is not directed to the incidental mischief that might occur in the course of a labor dispute; nor does it include peaceful picketing."

Because of these activities he now found himself precipitated into a dispute which was to hurtle him into the governor's chair. Governor Culbert Olson distrusted all Republicans, reasoning that their one objective was to defeat him at the next election. He knew very little about the character and background of Earl Warren, and very soon he came to the conclusion that the Attorney General's movements throughout the state were aimed at building a political machine which would enable Warren to supplant him in 1942. Since in his opinion the Democratic party was the party of the people in California, and since Republican Warren was his only potential opposition, he decided to cut down the Attorney General's influence. He feared the military, suspecting that it might be used against labor in times of strike, and looked with a jaundiced eye on his attorney general's meetings with the Army, Navy and F.B.I., and his efforts to integrate them with the state's law-enforcement agencies. When Warren asked the legislature for funds with which to continue his training and organizational work, and secured the passage of a good appropriation bill, Governor Olson vetoed the measure, effectively hamstringing Warren's efforts.

Thus developed the ironic situation in which Governor Olson, himself a completely honest and sincere man, by his own effort created the only opposition that could possibly have arisen to his re-election. For Earl Warren had no ambition to become governor.

"I am an advocate by nature," says Warren. He loved the law, he enjoyed judicial procedure, and he wanted to complete his job of rewriting the state's antiquated legal structure. He took pride in a job well done, and thought he would like to remain in this office for the rest of his life, or until some young, vigorous and successful district attorney came along and said, "Mr. Attorney General, whenever you decide to retire from this job please let me know, as I'd like to take it over when you are finished."

Nor was Governor Olson's quarrel with Warren the only one that had arisen in the capitol. Olson was at war with his legislature, even though the people of the state had sent a Democratic majority to Sacramento. He believed in a strong executive who told the legislative branch, always in the best interests of the state, just what laws and appropriations it should pass. He had had little experience in dealing with legislators, probably the most difficult art in the entire practice of democracy. The legislators wanted to be independent and pass their own legislation in their own way. By the end of his first year in office, Governor Olson's acrimonious attitude turned into a feud, with the Assembly and Senate refusing to pass good bills, even ones which they wanted, because he had originated them. The capital was torn with personal bitterness and strife among the state officers, with its resulting cliques, suspicions, accusations, backbiting and the refusal of half the branches of the government to cooperate with the other half. The atmosphere inside the capitol itself became one of tension, rancor and fear, with a deadly pall overhanging the whole political structure of the state.

When the Japanese attacked Pearl Harbor on December 7, 1941, Attorney General Warren was completely prepared. His office began operating on a twenty-four-

hour schedule in close cooperation with the armed services and the federal government. Within a week, working with the representatives of the cities and counties,
he had drafted the Blackout Ordinance which was
quickly passed by the legislature and served the state for
the duration of the war.

As a result of his study of saboteurs in Europe, he
conceived it his duty to prepare a statewide chart indi-
cating where the Japanese in California lived and where
they owned property, including its proximity to factories, shipyards and defense plants. He turned this
study over to the armed forces for their use and guid-
ance, appearing before the Army Commander in San
Francisco and the Tolan Congressional Committee.
When the General DeWitt Order took the Japanese out
of their homes and sent them to prepared camps far
away from important military installations, Warren de-
fended the constitutionality of the act on the grounds
that in time of war the military authorities had the
right to determine who could and who could not remain
in a strategic zone.

On the other hand, when Governor Olson's personnel
board took off the state's civil service availability lists
the names of people whose parents had been born in
Germany or Italy or Japan, Warren issued an opinion
that their civil rights must be protected, and that they
could not be taken off the lists or kept out of jobs by
civilian authorities.

Governor Olson had been building a State Guard
which now had some six thousand members under pay.
Warren concluded that since there were more officers
than enlisted men in the Guard, and since it was ineffi-

ciently administered, it could be of little help in times of emergency. He therefore requested the Governor to call the legislature into special session in order to pass laws which would make legal, and provide funds to, the many voluntary agencies he had set up during the past year, and put into effect such things as the State Fire Disaster Plan, giving the local councils of defense statewide authority.

Governor Olson called the special session of the legislature, but limited its deliberations to a request for seventeen million dollars to expand his State Guard, and an emergency fund of some four million dollars to be spent at his discretion. The session developed into a battle between the Governor and the legislators, who gave him only a portion of the sum he wanted both for the Guard and his own emergency fund.

Under the limited call the legislature was prohibited from discussing any of the matters that the Attorney General deemed urgent, or passing laws which would enable the local defense councils to function. Nor would Olson summon together the State Council of Defense, the integral parts of which had been so well organized. The group had declared its need and intention of meeting once a month, but it couldn't proceed in the face of the Governor's opposition.

Then came the climax of the contest between the Governor and his attorney general, a contest which arose out of the character of both men. Under the Disaster Relief Act of 1923, which covered such calamities as fire, pestilence and flood, the Governor of California was enabled to appoint men with the highest police powers to act in the distressed areas. Olson now interpreted this act as giving him the right to name his State Guard officers, all of whom he had appointed, to head each major locality in the state, with complete power to rule over the local authorities. Olson announced this decision at the first open meeting of the Legislators Defense Council in Sacramento. Earl Warren was thoroughly aroused, for this attitude violated his basic concept of cooperative government in which the local citizens and the local elected authorities governed themselves. He informed the Governor that the Disaster Relief Act of 1923 specifically exempted war, and passed around copies of the statute to prove his point. Then he added, "There is only one way for the Governor to supplant the local authorities, and that is to declare martial law. There has been no call for martial law. Any effort on the Governor's part to declare martial law will be illegal, and as attorney general, I will consider it my duty to fight it."

This meeting proved to be the final parting of the ways for the elected governor and the elected attorney general of the state. Governor Olson decided that he must rule through personal decree in this hour of emergency. Attorney General Warren believed the exact opposite. He refused to assume any power for himself or his office which was not clearly delineated in the laws or the constitution of the state. From that moment on the Governor invited Warren to no more meetings, and completely bypassed the attorney general's office, asking him no legal opinions, and providing no funds out of his emergency appropriation with which to implement the local defense organizations.

The state's volunteer defense forces fell into such a

confused, ineffective state that James Landis, Federal Director of the Office of Civilian Defense, said, "California's failure to adopt a legislative program to meet the war problems has caused California to lag behind the eastern states."

Having taken all power and function out of his hands, Governor Olson had left the Attorney General sitting in his spacious corner office with literally nothing to do. Earl Warren, now fifty years old, with enormous vitality, a love of good work, and with a passionate devotion to his country's welfare in the tragic hour of weakness and military defeat, had three choices before him: he could sit in this office twiddling his thumbs; he could resign and leave the sordid mess behind him; or he could throw his whole heart and energy into the task of supplanting Olson, and help to make California a great war state.

His decision didn't take very long to resolve itself. One afternoon he jumped up suddenly from his desk, slapped his hat on his head, drove across the San Francisco Bay Bridge and went home to his wife. Once inside the door he said:

"Nina, I am going to have to run for governor. I know that I have only an outside chance, I know that if I am defeated our whole lives will be changed, and that I will have to find some other form of activity, but I simply cannot sit in that office another hour without an important war job to do."

Nina Warren smiled gently and replied:

"Well, Earl, if that's what you feel you have to do, then that's what we have got to do."

That night Warren made his decision known to a group of friends. They were aghast. "Oh, no, Earl," they protested. "You can't do that now. You can't beat Olson and that Democratic machine. Wait another four years and then you will have a good chance."

It was not a good chance that Warren was looking for. When he said that he was determined to try, they answered, "Will you give us time to take a poll? We're sure a poll will convince you."

"Go ahead, but I warn you that I am going to make the effort even if the polls are heavily against me."

They were. Only nineteen percent of those queried indicated that they would vote for Earl Warren; some thirty-nine percent said they would vote for Olson. When he saw the results of the poll, Warren pointed to the more than forty percent of the voters still undecided.

"I'm going after them."

During the next months his friends and admirers among the Republicans in San Francisco got together a campaign fund with which to pay for literature, mailing, posters, radio time and rallies. However the wealthy Republicans of Southern California decided that Warren's case was hopeless, and that they therefore would not contribute anything to his fund, but would devote their money and efforts to electing a Republican legislature.

Warren filed on both the Republican and Democratic tickets. Then, with his good friend Leo Carrillo, the movie actor, whose family had been in California long before its inception as a state, he set out in an open car to tour the vast distances of California. They would

pull into a small town, stop the car at the main intersection, then Carrillo would exhort the passers-by to
gather around. After he had warmed up the crowd
with a few laughs he would announce that he was of
California ancestry under three flags, that he loved the
state dearly, and that in wartime he felt a man like Earl
Warren could give the people the united and cohesive
spirit so needed in emergencies. Warren then spoke to
them of the causes which underlay California's confused
civilian defense effort, told them why he was running
for governor, and what his program would be.

They spent the better part of three months riding the
dirt roads, and visiting the inland communities, trying
to cover every square mile in the state. Warren went
into the shipyards, airplane factories, fruit-packing
plants, oil refineries, lumber mills, talking to the working men at lunch time, meeting literally tens of thousands of Californians. Most of the voters believed him
when he said he was nonpartisan: that he had been a
nonpartisan attorney general for four years, and had
every intention of being a nonpartisan governor, managing the state for the people and the war effort, and
not for any political party. This was made easier to
accept when the people throughout the state saw that he
had no rich machine behind him but only such friends
and enthusiasts as he could earn while he went along.

Several times he was told pointedly that his bid for
nonpartisan support was being resented in certain conservative circles, and was drying up the most fruitful
sources of campaign contributions. Warren smiled whim-
sically, and said:

"If contributions are not forthcoming, we will manage to campaign in our own way without them."

He was helped among the independent voters by the fact that he looked, sounded, felt like an honest and able man.

Sixteen years before, when making his first political canvas, he had said, "I got elected district attorney by meeting and talking to more voters than any candidate had before." This tactic very nearly worked again in the 1942 primaries, for neither Olson nor any of his advisers had taken Warren seriously, and Olson had done no campaigning. When the primary ballots were in, Warren had received 635,230 Republican votes, and 404,778 Democratic votes. Olson had gathered only 514,144 votes out of the 2,242,901 registered Democrats in the state, a margin over Warren of only 110,000 votes for the Democratic nomination! Warren's Southern California campaign fund had been made of five- and ten-dollar bills contributed by young professional men and small businessmen; it had not quite added up to enough to mail out letters to the voters stating the case for Warren. If there had been sufficient funds in Southern California, it is very possible that Warren would have secured the extra fifty-five thousand and one votes which would have defeated Governor Olson in the primaries.

The state was stunned by this development. Those who said that Warren didn't have a chance now climbed on the bandwagon. In November he defeated the incumbent Olson by almost three hundred and fifty thousand votes.

X. Era of Good Will

ON THE first day of his new job, Earl Warren walked along the ground floor of the state capitol until he came to his quarters. He stood before the big door with his head cocked to one side as he looked at the block printing over the door: THE GOVERNOR. "Hu'um," he murmured to William Sweigert, who had become his executive secretary, "sounds a bit pretentious, don't you think?" That afternoon the word THE was painted out. The sign now reads simply GOVERNOR. Warren feels more comfortable with it that way.

He did not pitch in at once to take care of the most important affairs of state, but instead spent the first few mornings becoming acquainted with the people with whom he would be working for the next four years, going from department to department, introducing himself, shaking hands, chatting in a leisurely and friendly fashion, learning the names and personalities of his neighbors. Even the secretaries in the remotest offices found that the new Governor remembered their names, had a smile and booming hello, and a question or two to ask about their families and interests each time he saw them.

An aura of good will returned to the government halls. The accumulated tensions began to dissolve and the surroundings to reflect the vibrant warmth of Warren's nature. The people of Sacramento, and the large numbers who had to go to the state capital for business purposes, began to say, "Nobody hates anybody around here any more."

In some measure this was because Earl Warren made a conscious effort to restore simple human dignity and equanimity to the capital, but in larger measure it was because he liked people, and wanted people to like him. It had been his lifetime conviction that in democratic government it is the morale of the people that is most important; that when the citizens of a community like each other, nothing serious can happen to them.

The people who work in Governor Warren's office do so in an atmosphere of respect and confidence. They say, "The Governor builds us up. When we have a problem, when we are confused or troubled, we go into his room and in his calm way he indicates a course of action. He doesn't tell us when we've done a good job, he expects that of us, but we hear from others that he has been bragging about the fine results we've been getting."

From the beginning he resolved to get the best men in the state to head the various departments. Public health had always been one of his strongest interests, and everywhere he went during these early days he asked, "Who is the most able man in California to become the Director of the State Department of Public Health?" Doctors and laymen alike answered, "Dr. Wilton L. Halverson,

Health Officer of Los Angeles County . . . but you would
never be able to get him." Warren went down to see
Dr. Halverson, indicated his ambitious plans to give California the most modern and scientific public health program in the country, and then told Dr. Halverson that
everyone agreed that he was the right man to handle the
job. Halverson accepted at once, even though it meant
a substantial reduction in personal income.

As Director of Public Works he appointed Charles Pur-
cell, who had been in the highway department for years,
and had been doing the actual work of highway engineering; the employee who had been doing the major part of
the work in the narcotics department was made its director. He asked the Federal Reserve Bank officials to
recommend a man to head the Building and Loan Commission and appointed their choice; when he wanted to
put a C.I.O. man on the pension committee he called the
C.I.O. and named their choice. In order to keep the
courts functioning at their highest possible level he submitted all his proposed judicial appointments to the State
Bar of California, though the law did not oblige him to
do so.

He studied the records of the Olson appointees, and
when they were good men he not only retained their services, but, as in the case of Director of Agriculture William Cecil, reappointed them to head their departments.

Among the most delicate of all positions to fill was that
of Commissioner of Public Utilities, the difficulty being
to get a man who would not polish apples with the telephone, gas and electric, water and railroad companies he
was supposed to regulate. After very long study Warren
decided that Harold Anderson, the head of Palo Alto's

Municipal Department of Light and Power, was his man. Anderson at first declined, but Warren persuaded him that there was a great opportunity for broadened public service and that he would be completely free to act according to the dictates of his judgment. Anderson had not been on the commission very long when the Pacific Gas and Electric Company decided to float a large bond issue. A single investment banking house in San Francisco had had a monopoly on the underwriting of all such bonds. Commissioner Anderson decided that for the first time there would be competitive bidding for the issue. When this news was announced someone told the Commissioner, "You can't do that. Don't you know that such-and-such a firm contributed to Warren's campaign fund? The Governor will want you to hand over the issue to them."

When Anderson reported this scene to the Governor, Warren replied:

"When anyone tells you what I will or won't do, invite him in here to say those things in front of me. You can go back to your office and do your job the way you think it should be done in the public interest."

There are about a thousand important state positions in California which the governor must fill, but less than a hundred of them are full-time, paid jobs. The others, which consist for the most part of memberships on the state's numerous boards and commissions, must be filled by scientific or professional men and women who are occupying full-time jobs in their own fields, and serve the state at considerable sacrifice of time and income, their only reward being the satisfaction of giving public service. Warren spent months searching out top men, and few first-rate people ever turned him down.

On the other side of the shield is the story of the prominent Republican, a man of considerable means, who had backed Warren both hard and ably in the gubernatorial campaign. When Warren was elected, the backer went about his little community telling his friends that the Governor was going to appoint him to the fish and game commission, an appointment which carried no compensation but on which the man had set his heart. Warren investigated his background and found that, aside from liking to fish and hunt, he had neither experience nor training in the highly scientific problems of fish and game development and conservation.

When Warren refused to make the appointment his backer cried, "But Governor, you can't do this to me. I've already told my friends I'm going to get the appointment. Surely you wouldn't embarrass me?"

"You have already embarrassed me," replied Warren. "It is my duty in the public interest to appoint men to the fish and game commission who are trained in the field."

"But I'm as qualified as Smith and Jones, who have served on the commission in the past."

"True," replied Warren, "but those were not my appointments. I've got to get the most valuable men in the state to serve on the commissions. As soon as an opening comes up in a field where I know you are qualified I shall appoint you."

Mrs. Warren faced an equally difficult job of restoration. Not for many decades had a large family occupied the governor's mansion in Sacramento; most of the former governors had been older men, whose families were grown, and who maintained homes in the cities from which they had come. For the greater part they rented suites in the Senator Hotel in which to live while serving in Sacramento. The old wooden house which the state had purchased many years before was in almost a complete state of collapse. Everything above the second story was boarded up and decaying, the columns and porticos rotted, the porches in some instances broken through. The mansion, with its hundreds of curlicues, spires and dormers, had been built in the 1870's by a millionaire miner and later had been owned by Lincoln Steffens' family. It had not been renovated for a very long time, the wallpaper was hanging in strips, the furniture and carpeting were moth-eaten.

The state's historical organizations were delighted with the Governor's determination to reestablish the dignity and importance of the executive mansion. When Nina Warren first stopped in front of the moribund building her heart sank. But Earl wanted to bring his family here, to make this a real home so that his children might grow up in the community and he could spend the whole year in the very midst of the state government. She rolled up her sleeves and pitched in.

The legislature gave her a modest appropriation to put the mansion back in shape; Oscar Jahnsen, who had become one of the Governor's aides, supervised crews of carpenters, plumbers, electricians and painters. Mrs. Warren, a woman of inexhaustible energy and fine taste, shopped throughout the state to get the best bargains in Sarouk rugs, quiet but elegant wallpapers, velvet hangings, rich fabrics with which to cover the divans, and to fill in the sets of French glassware and Spode china which had been left in fragments in the old kitchen. The task required months of work, but by the time the six Warren children moved in, the mansion was livable, warm and cheerful, having recovered much of its original grace.

It did not take Nina Warren long to become California's First Lady. When a thousand Girl Scouts came for tea she refused to serve them in paper cups because she wanted the children to find in the governor's mansion an exciting glamor and elegance. This was not easy; she had assumed the position of official hostess of the state during the war years. With six young children, four flights of stairs and some twenty-odd rooms, domestic help was hard to keep, and there were tragicomic moments when the cook or serving maid walked out just as the wives of the legislators were coming in to lunch, or the cabinet and Supreme Court arriving for dinner.

Governor Warren's first inaugural address before his legislature was short and simple. He told the assemblage that their immediate task was to restore a spirit of unity in the state government so that California could play its full part in the war emergency. He assured them that he wanted to work with them and that he wanted them to work with him. With almost his first words he expressed his concern over the problems of public health which had already arisen with the influx of some three million people into the state to man the huge new war industries and till the fields.

The War Powers Act which he submitted to the legislators, giving the governor broader authority in times of crisis, was quickly passed by both houses. As governor he still disbelieved in strong central power, even though he would now be the one to administer it.

"I have never tried to centralize power in the state government," says Warren. "Even when I advocate new functions, we decentralize to give as much autonomy to local agencies as is consistent with good management. I believe in this as a principle of government. The federal government, as well as the state, should interest itself in employment, health, education, but the administration of these matters should be kept close to the people."

It had been the custom of all California governors to appoint a floor leader or whip who introduced to the legislators the bills in which the Governor was interested, rounded up and bargained for votes and wielded the political pressure needed to force the legislature to do what the Chief Executive wanted. Warren refused to use this device.

"The executive and legislative branches," he said, "must develop a policy of mutual respect and separate responsibility."

Instead he made his recommendation in his legislative message. In order that there should be no misunderstanding of his meaning, he had the bills prepared and offered for introduction to legislators who had shown an interest in the subject matter and who could be relied upon to work for their enactment. As a contrast to the usual stiff gubernatorial appearances to which the legislators were accustomed, Warren occasionally walked onto the floor unannounced and moved from desk to desk chatting with the lawmakers.

Both houses were lost at first, unused to so much looseness and freedom, but Warren's policies soon began to pay off: the legislators passed over ninety percent of his announced program during his six years in office. Only

once in that period was his veto overridden, and only two
of his important recommendations remained unenacted.

Unlike Olson, who had virtually abandoned the practice, he once again held regular meetings with his cabinet
to which he invited the attorney general and the reporters. He never held a conference or important meeting
without inviting the press. If this frankness made it hard
on the politicians, it also made for well-considered state-
ments. The door to the Governor's office is so wide open
that anyone sitting in an anteroom can, by only slightly
straining his ears, hear everything being said across Warren's desk.

This same spirit now became useful in his work with
private pressure groups. He was not afraid of opposition
but he never invited a fight. He said to angry and dis-
gruntled groups, "I will go along with you to remove the
inequity, but you have to show me an alternative."

In the case of the Truck Tax Repeal Bill, which was
twice passed almost unanimously by the legislature, but
which Warren twice vetoed, a group of fifteen owners
of large trucking fleets appeared in Warren's office with
fire in their eyes. They came out a half-hour later smiling
and saying, "We had a nice visit with the Governor. We
saw some points we hadn't thought of. Maybe we have
made some mistakes, but now we feel everything can be
ironed out." They had lost their bitterness because they
saw that the Governor was not being arbitrary or influenced by outside pressures, but had an honest and decent
position in the matter. He hadn't closed the door to the
truckmen or to discussion, and he was honestly looking
to them to find a way out of the dilemma.

He had worked steadily to raise the wages of teachers, increase their pensions and get an allocation of state funds to the poorer counties so that the teachers and school systems might be helped. "The teachers who take care of our young children are often paid less than our janitors," said Warren.

Then the teachers, after much hard work, managed to push a bill through the legislature in their own behalf. It was an important bill for them because it involved their state retirement fund out of which pensions are paid. Warren felt that the bill was badly written, that it had been conceived in haste, did not make adequate provision for the protection of the retirement fund and did not operate equitably between the rural and city teachers. He called in the representatives of the teachers to tell them that he felt he had to veto the bill and why he was doing so. He then advised them to go back home, think the matter over carefully and write a bill which would accomplish their purposes better, assuring them that he would later call a special session to deal with their proposed legislation. The teachers were bitterly disappointed and went away angry. Many observers considered it poor politics to veto a major bill supported by a teachers' organization. However, after studying the matter and getting competent legal counsel, the teachers rewrote the measure to meet the Governor's objections. Warren then kept his promise; he called a special session to reconsider the matter, and when the new bill was passed he signed it with the greatest pleasure.

The machinery of state government, which had been left unchanged for many years, was now given a thor-

ough overhauling by Warren, just as he had reorganized
the district attorney's office and the attorney general's
office. The duties of all departments were brought into
their proper relationship, and overlapping, duplication
and waste were quickly spotted and rooted out.

The California prisons, which had been operated under
an antiquated system, with no central director over the
various wardens, were brought under a single director of
corrections, Warren asking the federal government to
lend him its best men to help set up the new system. The
new wardens were appointed only after rigorous examination and, with their entire staffs, brought under civil
service. The parole board was also taken out of politics
and turned over to trained criminologists working on a
full-time basis. And at last his plan which enabled paroled men to earn their full pardon was put into effect.

The condition of the mental institutions within the
state was a disgrace. The asylums were overcrowded;
when the Governor made his inspections he found old
people sleeping on the higher floors and in the corridors
of firetraps. The inmates had little opportunity to secure
the benefits of modern therapy or psychiatry. Outraged,
he had new ground cottages built for the unfortunates,
and acquired two hospitals from the Army for their further protection. He converted the antiquated Department of Institutions into a modernized Department of
Mental Hygiene, saying, "We must take California out
of the asylum age and put it in the hospital age."

The legislature voted him funds; for the first time an
adequate staff was introduced and the latest scientific
methods made available to the patients.

Meanwhile Sacramento had a fine time absorbing the

Governor's large and friendly family. After dispatching
the last of the children to school and feeding his springer
spaniels, Governor Warren walked the mile down to the
capitol, giving a hearty "good morning" to his neighbors
as he passed. He never went straight to his desk but always took a complete turn around Capitol Park in which
are planted representative trees from each nation in the
world, chatting with the gardeners about the flowers and
the condition of the old trees which needed propping. At
lunchtime if he had an important guest or press representative, he would walk him over to the Sutter Club,
otherwise he would come down the short corridor of his
own little group of offices calling out to Bill Sweigert, his
press secretary Verne Scoggins or whoever else might be
free, "Let's go to lunch. Where'll we eat?" usually ending
up in a little Mexican restaurant having a tamale, or a Chinese restaurant where he ordered chow mein ". . . without
those little chopped onions, please."

After lunch he would stroll again in the state park for
a few minutes, with his face in the sun. Whenever there
was a spare day in the winter he took the children up to
Donner Pass for skiing. Frequently of a warm evening
he went out to the Barbara Worth Riding Academy with
Honey Bear and Bobby to watch them put their ponies
over the jumps, for the two youngest Warrens had been
growing up. Bobby, the only member of the family who
could talk his father out of anything, had developed a
rugged persistence which resulted in his converting a fat
little cow pony into a prize jumper. Every Wednesday
evening he could be found stretched out on the floor in
front of the radio, listening to *Mr. District Attorney*.
Young Nina, or Honey Bear, was the affectionate mem-

ber of the family.   Like Bobby, she had a large accumu-
lation of ribbons for expert riding and jumping.

In the summers the family occupied a cabin at Santa
Monica where they swam, fished and hunted grunion
when the tide and moon were right.   The Governor has
always remained an ardent follower of the University of
California football team; he remembers every exciting
play from Roy Riegels' Rose Bowl run in the wrong direction to the time when the baldheaded man sitting in
front of him grew so exasperated that he ran out on the
field and tackled Tom Harmon on California's ten-yard
line.

Earl Warren is mildly proud of his tall, broad figure,
and drapes it handsomely in well tailored double-breasted
suits.   The remnants of the old southpaw wildness can
now be detected only in the gay, bright patterns of his
neckties.

Mrs. Warren is the fiction reader for the family; the
Governor leans toward history, biography, international
politics, studies on management, labor and production.
He is not an omnivorous reader; he reads perhaps the
twenty most important books published each year, but
absorbs them so thoroughly that they become part of his
life.   He has always preferred experience and listening,
and has rather more instinctive wisdom than book learning.   His copy of the Bible never leaves the nightstand in
his bedroom and he reads it every night before going to
sleep.   The mainsprings of his character are spiritual
rather than intellectual.

XI. Portrait of a Governor

WHEN Earl Warren became governor in January of 1943, the organization he had put together while attorney general came to life. A new state war council which he set up immediately with the legislature, left to the local government agencies as much authority as possible to manage the war effort of their communities. They established their own voluntary services for fire watching, blackout ordinances, Red Cross, first aid and hundreds of other kinds of emergency relief. Every branch of the state government cooperated with the armed forces to insure all safety regulations and to facilitate the training of the millions of soldiers, sailors, fliers and marines who were stationed in California or embarked from its ports. Warren got rid of the makeshift, expensive State Guard and established a new and voluntary Guard which operated through the communities themselves, at about a tenth of the cost. In this work he was enthusiastically assisted by the League of Cities, composed of nearly three hundred cities and towns. This decentralized defense organization lent strength to the local governments. Although the latter

knew best their own problems and personnel, they were
helped by keeping in constant touch with every other
local group and knowing that the state government and
its full resources were behind them at every move.

The Governor did not try to manage everything himself, but created special agencies, like the Agricultural
Council, through which the farmers were able to recruit
and house the farm labor needed to harvest the vast
crops. California was also one of the most important
states in the Union in the quantity and variety of its war
production: planes from Lockheed and Douglas, ships
from Henry Kaiser's yards, armaments parts, explosives,
petroleum, timber, agricultural and dairy products.
California's population grew from seven millions to ten
millions, the most amazing growth in America's history.
The facilities for housing, education, public health and
law enforcement bulged past the breaking point. There
were shortages of food, housing, help. Yet California
lived at peace with itself, doing a monumental job of
war production, with an almost complete absence of
strikes, conflicts, feuds, hatreds. Whenever Earl Warren had taken an office he had performed as the servant
of all the people, and Californians now felt the complete
impact of his nonpartisanship as an abiding reality, not
a pose suddenly assumed in election campaigns. Over
the years he had built up a great reservoir of public confidence in his honesty, his integrity and fairness. The
people saw him appointing the best men available without regard to party, religion, race or creed. He was
criticized by implacable Tories on the right and equally
implacable Communists on the left; the other ninety-
eight percent of the people had confidence in their ad-

ministrator, and took from his attitude calmness, energy and tolerance. *Life* magazine has commented editorially: "Earl Warren managed California's vast prosperity without partisan politics."

He also managed it, even in the war crisis, on his original premise of decentralized authority. "The best war boards were local draft boards, operated on local levels and observing the equities," says Warren. "The people knew they were being judged by their neighbors. I asked the Superior Judges of the counties to name the best men for the draft boards and I always took their recommendations. I never had any trouble with the draft problem in California and I did not have to think about Selective Service five minutes a day. For the draft boards of appeal, I asked the judges of the appellate court of each district to recommend the board members. I doubt if we had more than three or four real complaints during the whole course of the war. This was a federal program, yet responsibility went right down to the neighborhoods. Most federal programs should, and could, operate this way."

In the one instance of racial conflict within the state, the street fights between service men and young Mexicans of Los Angeles wearing zoot suits, the Governor moved in four directions at once: he persuaded the armed forces to declare the Mexican quarters out of bounds; he requested the newspapers to get the stories and pictures off the front pages, where they were further inciting both sides, and onto the back pages in a few cold, non-inflammatory lines; he ordered Attorney General Robert Kenny to Los Angeles to command the law-enforcement officers and stop the violence; and he appointed a citizens' committee, headed by a Los Angeles bishop, to investigate the causes, and make recommendations to the Youth Authority. The zoot-suit riots lasted a few days and there never was a recurrence.

Warren initiated a program to make California a modern and progressive state. At his very first legislative session he raised pensions for old-age assistance from forty to fifty dollars a month, and by 1947 they were increased to sixty. At the same time he put through a fifteen-percent tax cut, saying, "I am satisfied that in government, as in all other affairs of life, it is not so much the size of the steps that determine progress as it is the direction in which the steps are taken." These tax reductions have amounted to five hundred million dollars during his incumbency.

He reorganized the Department of Industrial Relations to speed up the handling and disposition of workmen's compensation accident claims; broadened the unemployment-insurance system to take in employees of small establishments; increased unemployment benefits and shortened the waiting period from two weeks to one; secured increased workmen's compensation for the injured and for the widows and children of men who were killed; installed a practical conciliation service so that the state could go into a labor dispute when either side asked for it; asked the legislature to set up a school of industrial relations for labor and management at the University of California to give scientific training to both sides in the process of collective bargaining.

On another front, he rid the civil-service boards of politicians and put in trained personnel experts; placed

the deputies of the attorney general's office under civil
service; persuaded the legislature to vote money for
poorer school districts in order that they might build
modern schoolhouses; and installed a new recreation
commission to work with the cities to make it possible
for average income families to enjoy outdoor vacations.
He won funds to buy more state beaches and park areas,
and to open mountain trails for riding and hiking. He
established uniform rules of procedure for all state boards
and commissions which previously had had the right to
summon offenders, and act as investigator, judge and
jury. Warren said, "That savors of the kangaroo court,"
and installed impartial referees to preside over hearings,
thus insuring fair treatment to both the accused and the
board. This reform had long been advocated by the
American Bar Association as a sure method of eliminat-
ing the abuses of bureaucracy.

He secured millions of dollars to establish child-care
centers for infants and school children of employed
mothers. He obtained appropriations for spastic children, additional funds for the blind and the tubercular;
he got through the legislature a bill to establish a large
medical center in the University of California at Los
Angeles, and to match the money put up by the cities
and counties for more hospital facilities. In agriculture
he set up a statewide research commission to give the
farmers a grass-roots program for scientific packaging,
marketing and raising a healthy, profitable crop. He
secured the first legislation in the history of the state to
bring about conservation of the timberlands and their
reforestation for perpetual yield, so that trees could be
farmed in the same way as other crops. Because Cali-

fornia is a state-on-wheels, with a frightening annual death rate from accidents, he secured a ten-year program calling for an eighty-million-dollar annual expenditure to straighten and broaden the state's main arteries.

His work with Dr. Halverson for the public health is illustrative of the modern, scientific methods which he introduced into every department in the state. Experts from the Rockefeller Foundation were called in to survey the department as it had existed up to Warren's inauguration, and to set up what the Foundation considered would be the best possible structure and program for public health. With this reorganization effected, the public health department established a statewide plan of health education as an integral part of every school curriculum. Rigorous inspections of all foodstuffs, restaurants and sewage systems were initiated, with immediate suits brought against any localities contaminating either their own or near-by waters. A bill was passed obliging every hospital to secure a state license; close hospital supervision brought up sharply the standards of these institutions. State financial help was offered to those communities whose health standards were low, on condition that they use these funds to bring themselves up to the state standards. Infectious diseases were watched closely and epidemics reduced to the barest possible minimum. There was no phase of the public health in California which was not touched upon and improved by the public health department.

California had been the first to adopt the Youth Authority Plan recommended by the American Law Institute; however the California Authority had been on such a precarious footing that Warren's first legislature was ready to abandon it. The Governor's greatest interest had always been in children, and he now went to the legislature with probably the most impassioned appeal of his career, asking that funds be allocated and the Youth Authority be allowed to continue according to his own plan of reorganization. Prior to this time when boys or girls got into trouble they were quickly dispatched to institutions where many of them were ruined for life. Under Warren's proposal instead of holding a delinquent child in the county jail and then sending him to an outmoded reform school, officials committed him to the Youth Authority, where he was examined thoroughly from both the medical and psychiatric viewpoints. The Youth Authority then had a scientific as well as a humane basis on which to decide to which of the state's five correction homes the child should be sent for his greatest protection. Outdoor camps were created for both boys and girls, where they worked and played while being given excellent supervision and the training which would save them as citizens. The Youth Authority, when invited by cities and counties, made surveys of the causes of delinquency and helped the localities work out preventive programs.

In his appeal to the legislature in 1943 Warren said, "This is one of the greatest social experiments we have ever undertaken in this state." Since then his Youth Authority Plan has been adopted in such progressive states as Minnesota, Wisconsin and Massachusetts. In a book by John R. Ellingston, *Protecting Our Children From Criminal Careers,* John D. Rockefeller III, who provided the funds for the original Youth Authority study, says, "The application of the enlarged concept in

California suggests that the Youth Authority idea may be one of the truly creative social instruments of our time."

Knowing that every death sentence would finally come to him for executive clemency, Warren did not wait until the appeal was made before he acquainted himself with the case. He had the attorney general's office keep the file up to date, and he knew the details when his clemency was sought, thus avoiding the need for hurried decisions. He commuted sentences when he thought the purpose of justice would be better served. The best example is that of the young Sacramento Negro who was convicted of kidnaping and rape. Troubled, Warren called in the presiding judge and foreman of the jury, asking them if the verdict would have been the death penalty if the assailant had been white. Satisfied by their answers that it would not have been, Governor Warren commuted the sentence to life imprisonment.

Labor has taken considerable satisfaction from his regime, not only because of his extension of social security and increase in industrial accident benefits, but because he led the fight against bills which would have abolished the eight-hour law for women and minors. He told the legislature, "I will not be a party to the repeal of legislation which has taken generations to get on the statute books. However, if you can work out a compromise short of repeal whereby we can relax the law for special wartime purposes, without anyone being injured, I will sign such a bill." When a bill of this type went into effect, Warren dispatched his industrial relations director to check every application; permission for extra work was granted only where women's and children's rights were not sacrificed. When the canners of Santa Clara Valley asked permission to work young girls through the midnight shift, the Governor said, "I think of my daughter Virginia walking home from a cannery at two in the morning and I realize that I don't want this for anyone's daughter." Permission was never granted.

Strikes were sharply reduced and the state mediation service secured amicable settlements of many disputes before they reached a work-stoppage crisis. The unions grew angry with him only twice, the first time when he signed a bill outlawing jurisdictional strikes, declaring that feuds within the unions not only hurt the public and management, but most of all injured the unions themselves, and consequently should be outlawed. Their second displeasure occurred when Warren refused their demand that he veto a permanent bill against secondary boycotts. A so-called "Hot Cargo" bill had been passed by an earlier legislature for the duration of the war. Warren, then attorney general, advised that the bill was of doubtful constitutionality. The temporary law was approved by the voters of the state in a referendum, and the question of its constitutionality was then pending before the state Supreme Court. Warren felt he could not properly sign the permanent "Hot Cargo" bill because of his previous legal opinion, and did not want to veto it because he believed the state would be better served if he allowed the matter of constitutionality to be settled by the courts rather than be put aside by his veto. He let the bill become law without his signature. Both labor and management were aroused, accusing him of

fence-sitting, until the Supreme Court shortly after-
ward declared the "Hot Cargo" legislation unconstitutional.

The statewide enthusiasm engendered by the work of
the public health service now led to the planning for the
realization of one of Warren's great dreams. He had
been brought up on the stories of how Methias' young
brother died because he had no money for doctors, hospitals or medicine. He had prosecuted with an almost
Olympian anger the fraudulent health-insurance rings
in Alameda County. Now as he studied the conditions
of the working people in the state he came to the conclusion that "the American working man can afford to
die far better than he can afford a serious illness." He
reasoned that in our economy people buy insurance
against their houses burning down or their cars being
smashed. Why then did it not make even better sense
for men to buy insurance against ill health, so that if this
kind of misfortune struck they would not lose their savings or their homes. He figured if a cent or a cent and a
half were taken out of the working man's dollar and this
were matched with a similar amount by the employer,
and the fund and the insurance were then handled by a
state commission of the kind which functioned so successfully in the field of industrial compensation, the
working people of the state would have advanced another step toward security. This would add to the public health of the state because adequate care would always be available to its citizens. Governor Warren had
many friends in the medical profession and he believed
that the doctors would help him work out a helpful
solution of this problem.

As was his policy, he then turned to the specialists for discussion and counsel. One of his closest associates says, "Warren is the best listener in the state. He focuses one hundred percent on what you are saying, instead of trying to think up answers."

In December of 1944, while preparing his program for the 1945 meeting of the legislature, he called on a physician friend, Dr. Phil Gilman, who was president-elect of the California Medical Association. He explained what he called his "prepaid medical insurance" idea to Dr. Gilman, who was interested enough to arrange a conference with the executive committee of the California Medical Association. At this luncheon meeting Governor Warren disclosed all his thinking on the subject, suggested a few general principles, and asked for cooperation and help. The doctors expressed their appreciation of the Governor's consulting with them before initiating any legislative program and agreed to call a special meeting of the House of Delegates of the C.M.A. to consider his proposal. This meeting, held a week later in Los Angeles, ended in a thoroughgoing denunciation of Warren's prepaid health-insurance idea.

The Governor was disappointed but determined to carry on the fight. He said to the legislature, "Such a program will pay dividends to everyone. It will relieve suffering and anguish in the home, it will increase efficiency in the shop and office, it will relieve our counties of much of their load of the indigent sick. It will help make our citizens a healthier and happier people. We do not want to put the medical profession on the public payroll nor do we want to deprive the individual of the right to select his own physician. The professional relationship of doctor and patient will be a matter of free choice; our major purpose is to spread the cost of medical care among all people of the state."

The California Medical Association quickly assessed its members to send a high-powered lobby to Sacramento to block the Governor's legislation, accusing him of advocating socialized medicine. The medical lobby kept his bill from coming onto the floor of the legislature. The C.M.A. claimed that working men had no trouble getting good doctors and that all the hardships lay in meeting high hospital costs. Governor Warren next submitted a second bill covering prepaid hospital insurance. The C.M.A. now stirred up the hospitals on the charge that this would mean socialized hospitals and once again defeated Warren's measure.

The only bill which Warren could get through this legislature was one which paid working men the same compensation when they were unemployed because of illness as they got when they were unemployed because there was no work. Only one other state, Rhode Island, had such legislation. Warren has never given up his fight for prepaid medical insurance for every man, woman and child, and has presented the program so persistently to the American people through magazine articles, radio broadcasts, and addresses to the public that it has now become part of the mainstream of America's progressive thinking.

The public servant who cannot keep people working together amicably is of little value to his community; by the same token, the one who doesn't know when to get up on his hind legs and do battle, is of no value at all.

Earl Warren served as host governor to the United

Nations Conference in San Francisco in the spring of 1945, welcoming the foreign delegations and discussing the problems of world peace with the representatives. The state legislature was also meeting during these months, and Warren couldn't leave Sacramento until four or five in the afternoon for the two-hour drive down to San Francisco. However he was eager to attend as many United Nations Conference meetings as possible and to study at first hand the complexities of international relations. Often he did not get back home until three in the morning, but he was in his office by ten the next day to receive any legislators who wished to confer.

The moment the DeWitt Order banning the Japanese from the West Coast was rescinded, Warren made every effort to speed their return to their homes. When vigilante violence broke out against the returning Japanese in Central California, the Governor put a stop to this gangsterism in twenty-four hours.

Warren's second heated contest resulted from his proposal that California's low tax on gasoline be increased, the money to be used to build new roads and to make safer the congested main arteries. The oil companies fought him on the grounds that added gasoline taxes meant a lesser sale of gasoline. Warren replied that in the American tradition better roads meant more driving and hence a greater sale of gasoline. Attacking obliquely, the oil companies combined to raise their own gasoline price uniformly so that the advance matched the added tax for which the Governor had asked. This was too much for even the conservative press of California, and when Warren took his fight directly to the people, dramatizing the fact that California killed more people on its highways than New York and Pennsylvania combined, he was backed by every newspaper and by the overwhelming weight of public opinion. Caught between the oil lobby on the one hand and the irate voters on the other, the legislature finally passed the bill.

The Republican platform during the presidential campaign of 1944 had promised the passage of Fair Employment Practices bills. Returning to California from the Republican convention in Chicago, Warren told the legislature, "During the war it has been illustrated that our people possess a desire to break down artificial barriers which give rise to demonstrations of racial prejudices. The accomplishment of this purpose will do more to insure lasting peace throughout the world than all other factors combined. What we strive to do in world affairs we should most certainly augment by practices here at home."

To accomplish this purpose, he introduced a bill calling for a Commission of Political and Economic Equality to study the existing conditions and statutes on discrimination and to suggest new laws and remedies.

California's leftists had no patience with this kind of careful, studious approach. A Los Angeles legislator introduced a bill which provided criminal penalties for employers who violated the proposed law. This bill was killed in committee and Governor Warren's bill with it. The following year an F.E.P.C. bill, sponsored by the C.I.O., was submitted to the people by an initiative petition, but the criminal penalty clause so frightened the voters they defeated the measure. Warren's continued battle for a sensible and workable Political and Economic Equality Law got him into trouble with both houses.

For the first time since the election of 1942 the Governor's supporters were saying, "If the legislators won't work with him, why doesn't Governor Warren take the boys over, threaten to veto their bills, use a whip in the legislature and make reprisals?"

These were not Warren's methods. He said to William Sweigert, "They may defeat us on these measures, they may make us look bad, even create a condition where we will be defeated at the next election. But we can walk out of here and know we do not have to lower our head or avert our eyes. We can feel that we have made a good, forthright pitch for what we feel is right."

The voters knew it too. When Warren stood for re-election in 1946 he was nominated in the June primaries by both the Republican and Democratic parties, and that was the end of the election. The Los Angeles *Daily News,* the only Democratic paper in Southern California, wanted desperately to back Republican Warren because they had heartily approved his administration; the only reason they didn't endorse him was, as one of the editors plaintively put it, "How can we claim to be a Democratic paper if we go around endorsing Republicans?"

Earl Warren was the first governor to be re-elected since Hiram Johnson in 1915, and only the third governor to be re-elected in the state's history. Never before had a California governor been given a mandate by both political parties. Warren did not use this startling fact to gather more personal power, but deliberately asked the legislature to terminate all war agencies and to strip him of the extra powers which had been granted him because of the emergency.

His opening message to the legislature on January 6, 1947, outlined one of the most forward-looking programs ever presented in this country. It was written simply and with utter clarity. When writing anything, the Governor asks himself, "Do I completely understand it? Do I really believe that? Will I believe it five years from now?"

Warren perceived that at the existing rate of growth California would be the second largest state in the Union by 1950. Because there had been little building during the war and schools, hospitals and youth centers were overcrowded and hard-used, he knew that a vast government building program would be necessary.

His budget for 1948 was the largest ever to be presented in any state legislature, a near-billion dollars to be expended in one year. Yet all of this work and building was to be done without the state going one cent into debt; three hundred million dollars had been put aside during the war years for just such postwar building, and the balance of some six hundred and twenty million dollars was to be derived from taxes. The Governor also asked that seventy-five million dollars of surplus be put away as a "rainy day fund" to cushion against a low state income due to a falling economy. About half of the state expenditures were to be reallocated to cities and counties to raise teachers' pay and old-age pensions, build badly needed schools, colleges, hospitals, parks, playgrounds and roads, implement public-health programs and make habitable the emergency veteran housing provided by the federal government.

Because of Warren's years of planning, the state was ready for any emergency which might arise from reconversion to a peacetime economy. However there was no economic distress, shutdown or unemployment; ironically enough, the Governor had to hold back on everything except imperative building so that the state would not contribute to inflation.

Articles appeared about his work in the *Saturday Evening Post, Collier's, Life, Time, Newsweek, Look, Better Homes and Gardens.* The Republican National Convention of 1944 had named him as its keynote speaker and he was urged to accept the vice-presidential position on the ticket with Governor Thomas E. Dewey of New York. Warren had then been governor for only a year and a half and was involved in the monumental task of converting California to a war economy. He wanted above all things to fulfill his promises, effectuate a liberal program and see California through the war. He declined the nomination.

Four years later in 1948, with the three war years behind him, the state enjoying prosperity and full employment, the story was different. His name was mentioned frequently as a prospective presidential nominee, yet aside from agreeing that the California delegation should put him in nomination, he made no organized effort to secure the nomination, nor would he allow anyone to solicit the support of delegates in other states or to collect campaign funds.

"I have made a distinction between being willing to

serve if called upon to serve and the position of being an
active candidate, which would take me away from my
job as governor and require me to solicit campaign
funds." He stuck to this resolution, refusing to enter
the primaries in any state, even in next-door Oregon
when invited to come in by the Republicans of that
state. When campaign checks for a thousand dollars
and five hundred dollars arrived from well-wishers,
Warren returned them with thanks, saying, "I wouldn't
know what to do with the money."

He went to Philadelphia with a loyal California delegation, but without any other visible support. They
took with them only Warren buttons and orange juice,
rather light artillery with which to besiege the giant
citadel of the presidency. There was the hope that if
the other leading candidates deadlocked, the convention
might agree upon Warren as acceptable to all. His
name was placed before the convention by Dr. Robert
Gordon Sproul, President of the University of California.

At the end of the second ballot, when Thomas E.
Dewey had five hundred and fifteen votes, and needed
only thirty-three more to secure the nomination, Warren wrote a letter to the California delegates releasing
them from their pledges to him and advising them that
if he were in their place he would vote for Thomas E.
Dewey.

At four o'clock the following morning, while Warren was asleep in his room at the Warwick Hotel, the
telephone rang. It was Governor Dewey asking if Governor Warren wouldn't please come immediately to his
headquarters at the Bellevue-Stratford. All during that

night Republican leaders had been reviewing the names and personalities of potential Vice Presidents: Halleck of Indiana, Bricker of Ohio, Martin of Massachusetts, Stassen of Minnesota and many others. Governor Dewey had listened and considered carefully everyone suggested. The only man upon whom all the leaders present could agree was Earl Warren.

When Warren reached Dewey's rooms at about four-fifteen, the New York Governor was alone. Dewey told Warren that he wanted him as his running mate. Warren replied:

"Tom, I can't spend my years just calling balls and strikes in the Senate."

"I wouldn't expect you to, Earl. I would want you to be a partner in the administration."

"Well, if it's to be a working job, I'm willing to do it."

Earl Warren was nominated by acclamation at noon on Friday, June 25, 1948. Neither his wife nor three daughters, who were sitting in Convention Hall, knew of his decision to accept until he came into the hall. Warren made a simple acceptance speech, filled with warmth and humor and humility. The delegates gave him an ovation. Governor Dewey said to the press:

"I am sure that Warren could be relieved of his Senate duties sufficiently so that he could give a large part of his time to the administration of our government. He will sit in the Cabinet and be a full partner."

XII. The Assistant Presidency

WHEN Earl Warren telephoned to California to tell his thirteen-year-old son Bobby that he had been nominated for Vice President, there was a moment of quiet on the line. Then Bobby asked:

"Is that good?"

The office of Vice President has long been an object of indifference and frequently of derision. John Adams, the very first to hold the job, under George Washington, wrote to his wife Abigail, "The vice presidency is the most insignificant office that ever the invention of man contrived." Thomas Jefferson, who succeeded Adams to the office, complained that it paid only five thousand dollars a year, "hardly enough to live on." John C. Calhoun, who served under Andrew Jackson, became so enraged at his enforced idleness and his inability to work for states' rights that he resigned from the vice presidency and returned to the Senate. Mrs. Calvin Coolidge, when told by her husband on the long-distance telephone that he had been nominated for Vice President, gasped, "Surely you're not going to take it!"

The best loved political joke of our times comes from

Of Thee I Sing, a musical satire by George Kaufman
and Morrie Ryskind, in which a group of tourists are
being shown the White House by a guide. Told that
this is where the President lives, one of the tourists asks,
"And where does the Vice President live?" Throttle-
bottom, the Vice President, emerges from the group of
tourists and replies meekly:

"In a boarding house over on Z Street."

The Constitution of the United States devotes only
one sentence to the actual duties of the Vice President.
Article I, Section 3, reads: "The Vice President of the
United States shall be President of the Senate, but shall
have no Vote, unless they be equally divided." This line
was written in 1787, and in the one hundred and sixty-
one years of our rapidly expanded commonwealth has
never been amended. Congress has passed only two
brief laws in all this time which refer to the office, the
first raising its salary to its present inadequate level, the
second naming the line of succession to the White House
in the event of the death of the Vice President.

Both Governors Dewey and Warren have said, "Democracy is not a static form of government." The office of the Vice President alone in American history has
remained completely static in function. It is incom-
prehensible that this office should have so long remained
neglected.

The contempt in which the vice presidency has been
held has contributed heavily to the sleazy, thoughtless
manner in which the vice-presidential nominees have
been chosen at the political conventions. Literally millions of columns of ink are spilled for months in ad-

vance of the conventions on the question of whom the
parties should choose for their presidential nominees,
but aside from considering whether this or that disappointed nominee might take the vice presidency as a
consolation prize, no newspaper analyst or commenta-
tor ever bothers to ask himself or the public who would
make the best Vice President.

By the time the delegates have selected their presidential nominee they are so exhausted by the speeches,
the heat, the repetitive roll call of states and the fever-
ish badgering that goes on outside the convention hall
that a considerable portion of them actually return
home before the selection of the vice-presidential candidate begins. Their attitude frequently is, "What possible difference can it make who sits up there in front
of the Senate and says, 'The Chair recognizes the Senator from North Dakota.' "

In a recently published book called *Heirs Apparent*
which contains the stories of all of our Vice Presidents,
the authors, Young and Middleton, comment acidly
that the vice-presidential nominee "must come from a
community as distant as politically feasible from the
bailiwick of the White House candidate, and must be,
as far as humanly possible, colorless and nondescript."
So successfully was this formula carried out in 1876
that after the Republicans had nominated Rutherford
B. Hayes for the presidency they gave him William A.
Wheeler as a running mate. Hayes asked more in sor-
row than anger:

"Who is Wheeler?"

There are exceptions; some few Presidents have utilized their Vice Presidents. William McKinley devel-

oped so much liking and respect for his Vice President, Garret A. Hobart, that he called him in for advice on business matters, legal problems and questions of governmental procedure. When the United States went to war with Spain in 1898, Hobart was asked to participate in Cabinet meetings. President Woodrow Wilson gave to Vice President Thomas R. Marshall the job of persuading the Senate to pass his World War I legislation. Franklin D. Roosevelt influenced the Democratic convention of 1940 to name Henry A. Wallace for the vice presidency. Roosevelt was not inclined to build up strong men, but the pressure of war work led him to make Vice President Wallace an ex-officio member of the Cabinet, chairman of several important commissions and an unofficial ambassador-at-large to represent the administration in Mexico, Europe, Russia and China.

Other relationships have gone all the way from mild annoyance on the part of the President to severe distaste. President Coolidge thoroughly disliked his Vice President, Charles G. Dawes, on the grounds that Dawes was loud, talkative and quarrelsome. Nor did stealing the limelight from his superior endear Dawes to the White House.

The first Vice Presidents were men of the highest caliber and the vice presidency served as an apprenticeship for the presidency. John Adams was elected President after serving for eight years as Vice President under George Washington; Thomas Jefferson was Vice President for four years under Adams before he was elected President; and Jefferson's Vice President, Aaron Burr, might also have become President had he not quarreled with Jefferson over the presidency. Since that time no Vice President has been elected to the presidency who has not already succeeded to the White House because of the death of a President. The tradition of the Vice President serving as an apprentice President may well be revived.

When Governor Thomas E. Dewey told the nation's press and radio, after his nomination in Philadelphia, that he believed the time had come to transform the office of Vice President into the office of what he described as "assistant president," with wide and important powers, he not only called attention to the greatest single need in the federal government today but also put into terms of workable political philosophy a sentiment which has been steadily growing in the minds of the Congress and the public. With the growth of the American population to more than one hundred and forty million people, and the vast expansion of the country's industry, the job of the President would be a killing one even if the United States were isolated between its Canadian and Mexican boundaries and its two oceans. Now that the United States has become one of the focal cores of international politics, the President's work on foreign affairs is more than enough to consume all of the energy and genius of any one man if the world is to be kept at peace. For future Presidents to attempt to administer both our vast domestic economy and our tremendous international obligations, without the active help of the Vice President, would be not only foolhardy but virtually impossible. It would be as inimical to the health of our government as it is to the health of the Chief Executive.

Never before has there been so great a need for an

assistant president or such an opportune and timely moment to accomplish this reorganization. However the revitalizing of the vice presidency must be done solely in the realm of domestic affairs, for the Constitution very clearly and categorically places the responsibility for foreign affairs in the hands of the President. It is equally clear from the Constitution that the Vice President cannot move into the legislative or judicial branches of the government, and that any and all of the duties assigned to him would have to be kept executive or administrative.

Since Governor Dewey's firm and convincing declaration that Governor Warren would become an assistant president and a full partner in his administration, every circle in American political life has been speculating on how this reorganization of the federal government can best be accomplished. Four possible methods have been evolved and are now being closely studied.

The first is by an executive decree setting forth the new functions and powers of the Vice President and allotting him certain funds from the President's emergency appropriations with which to carry out his duties. This approach has certain advantages: it can be accomplished quickly, without argument or effort at frustration by any other branch or agency of the government, and, if formulated by the President-elect in the days preceding his inauguration, can go into effect immediately upon his taking office. The role of assistant president could then be kept in a fairly fluid state, with more powers added by decree as the need arose. The assistant president would enjoy the authority and prestige which would come from the fact that the Chief Executive had taken this step of his own desire and volition.

There are also disadvantages to the executive-decree approach. Because this arrangement would be a purely personal one, no permanent structure could be established and no permanent duties set forth. Each newly-elected President would have different ideas on the scope and even the desirability of the assistant presidency. If the new office were left on so completely a voluntary basis, any President who did not wish to share his powers or who, unhappily, did not like the Vice President or, liking him, had no confidence in his ability to do the job, could summarily abolish the entire concept. Thus the work and effort put into the establishment of this office during a preceding administration would go down the drain. Good men who might be attracted to the assistant presidency if its duties were permanent and mandatory would be inclined to turn down the office if they knew that its larger function depended solely upon the decision, or even the whim, of the President.

An equally severe disadvantage of the executive decree is that it bypasses the Congress. While this might be entirely legal and within the powers of the President, it would have the inevitable result of antagonizing the Congress, which is ever zealous not only in preserving its rights but in seeing that no new agency functions for any length of time without its consent and its definition of the powers of the office. Thus estranged, the Congress, or at least individual congressmen, might well obstruct or even sabotage the work of the assistant president, failing to pass the legislation for which he might ask or refusing funds for any program he might suggest which could not be financed directly out of the President's funds. Moreover, if the assistant president's functions were created and delineated by executive decree, he might be resented or hamstrung by the Cabinet, whose members have been accustomed to dealing directly with the President. Franklin D. Roosevelt's Cabinet was not only offended by his bringing Henry Wallace into their confidential meetings, but actually tried to keep him out.

The Senate and the House might accept the Vice President as an assistant president through a second approach, that of having the Congress write the laws which create the office and at the same time define its functions. Any legislation passed by the Congress would have to authorize the President to assign to the Vice President, at his discretion, the duties described in the statutes. These laws could never compel the President to delegate powers to the Vice President. No President would sign this kind of mandatory law because it would strip him of his executive powers to such an extent that he would no longer be the Chief Executive. In addition, it would clearly be an invasion of the executive by the legislative branch and would probably be declared unconstitutional by the courts.

A discretionary statute might avoid these complications, might give the assistant presidency the prestige of having been authorized by the Congress, and at the same time leave the President free to determine for himself precisely how much and what kind of authority he wished to delegate to the Vice President. Thus the assistant presidency would be a contributory role and could never come into conflict with the presidency itself; neither could the assistant president, if he should prove unfriendly to the President, scuttle the President's domestic policy because he derived his authority from the Congress.

This second approach, by Congressional action, enjoys certain advantages. The President could initiate the measure himself, writing the bill to include whatever powers he was willing to delegate. The Congress could then rewrite the measure, reaching a working compromise with the President. Once Congress had passed these laws, the Vice President would probably be accepted in his new capacity.

The disadvantage of these laws, like that of the executive decree, is that they too tend to be temporary rather than permanent; each new President and Congress would want to redefine the office of assistant president, not in terms of its greatest potential in changing times, but rather in terms of the relationship between the new President and Vice President, and the new President and Congress. The highly explosive quotient of personality and party politics might be the determining factor of both the scope and effectiveness of the assistant presidency, rather than the urgency of the need for the office.

It would be more than difficult for the Vice President to work happily or effectively under these enabling laws, for he would know that the President could revoke his powers at any moment.

A third approach is based on the feeling in Washington that a Cabinet secretariat is needed not only to correlate the duties of the many departments and admini-

strative agencies but also to analyze and digest their
work and reports for submission to the President, so
that he may determine questions of policy and be relieved of the crushing burden of detail. To meet this
and other needs, the first session of the Eightieth Congress set up a commission on the reorganization of the
executive branch of the federal government. Former
President Herbert Hoover was asked by President Harry
S. Truman to head this commission. Mr. Hoover himself has taken over the investigation of the office of the
President, its relation to the various departments and
agencies of the government, and the major problem of
the revitalization of the office of the Vice President.

The first informal plan to emanate from political
circles was based on this idea of a Cabinet secretariat.
It has been suggested that the Vice President be placed
in charge of all domestic departments: Treasury, Justice, Interior, Commerce, Labor, Agriculture and Post
Office. This proposal has the advantage of freeing the
President to concentrate on foreign affairs, holding in
his hands the Departments of State and National Defense, and coming into the realm of domestic economy
only at the top policy levels. The President would
have the advantage of the Vice President's study and
findings of the various departments, and the Vice President, neutral and uncommitted to any one department,
could view objectively the position of the various
agency heads in relation to the whole organization of
the federal government.

The obstacles to this concept are that it might be difficult to get the best men in their fields if they knew
they could not work directly with the President. Again,

the cabinet officers might resent any intrusion of the Vice President into their domains, pointing out that the Congress had passed laws giving them the right to control their own departments. This is evidenced by former Secretary of the Interior Harold Ickes in his book, *My Twelve Years with FDR*, when he shows how he was able to defy not only the Secretary of State, but the President as well, when they wanted him to make helium gas available to Germany for her dirigibles.

These complications, difficulties and objections to the first three approaches have now led serious thinking to a fourth and highly feasible approach which, though it gives the Vice President considerably less scope and authority than the previous plans, would have the virtue of being an effective opening wedge in the reconstitution of the office and at the same time would avoid most of the objections and limitations of the first three methods.

It has been suggested that there be set up another executive department to be known as the Administrative Department which would encompass various agencies of government which are not now within any existing departments. For example, the Bureau of the Budget operates directly out of the President's office, and yet the President has little time to give it. The personnel and civil service agencies do not fall under the jurisdiction of any one cabinet officer. Neither does the vast operation of procurement of materials and supplies. All of these important functions could be combined into a single department of which the Vice President would be the head. He would be the Secretary of Administration and a member of the Cabinet.

Into the realm of the Secretary of Administration could fall the new programs which constantly arise, and do not by their nature fall logically within the jurisdiction of any older departments, springing as they often do out of needs which could not have been anticipated. Such programs could include the Atomic Energy Commission and the European Recovery Program which now operate directly under the President.

The Vice President would then be the only officer who would have an official capacity on both Capitol Hill and in the White House. One of the weaknesses of our federal government is that there is insufficient contact between the executive and legislative branches. In England the members of the Cabinet must be chosen from the Parliament, making for close contact between both these branches. In the United States the cabinet officers are exclusively executive officers and have no direct contact with the Congress. A Vice President who was popular with the Senate, over which he presides, could serve as the ideal liaison between the legislative and the executive, because he could bring the problems and requests of the Senate to the Cabinet, and the problems and requests of the Cabinet to the Senate. This dual capacity would inevitably bring him considerable influence in the Cabinet. If, added to this, his relationship with the President were good, he could wield a triple influence.

Because of the fact that such services as the budget, personnel, civil service, and procurement of materials and supplies reach down into every branch of the government, the Vice President would of necessity have an intimate acquaintance with every agency in Washington and a working knowledge of the extent and intricacies of the executive branch. A man with this training and background would be prepared to step into the White House if the need arose.

Because there is no reference in the Constitution to a cabinet, all existing departments have been created by legislative action at the request of the President, the laws clearly outlining the duties and functions of the new agencies. There is every reason to believe that the Congress would accede to the President's request for a new cabinet post, and create the office of the Secretary of Administration to be filled by the Vice President. This arrangement would be acceptable to both the President and the Congress. It would be equally acceptable to the Vice President because his duties would then be mandatory by statute, his job would be permanent within the term of his office and he would be free to work out a long-range program.

The single objection to this fourth approach is that the Vice President, as Secretary of Administration, would be the one cabinet officer whom the President could not fire. However if the Vice President had merely the status of another cabinet officer, with no jurisdiction over the Cabinet itself, amiable relations could be maintained.

Other minor obstacles which might prevent the best men from wanting to be Vice President are in process of being eradicated. The salary of twenty thousand dollars a year, which is less than that paid to the governors of New York or California or to the United States Supreme Court Justices, will probably be raised substantially. The Vice Presidents have suffered considerable discomfort and loss of social prestige because they have had no official dwelling in Washington. Bills have already been drafted in the Congress to make the historic and beautiful Blair House, now owned by the federal government and used by the Department of State to house visiting foreign dignitaries, the official residence of the Vice President. Another bill calls for a substantial appropriation with which to build a new and permanent home for the Vice President, and the allocation of funds which would enable him to relieve the President of much of the burden of official entertainment. Both parties have joined in drafting this legislation, which is of a nonpartisan nature.

The dual responsibility offered by the creation of an assistant presidency will attract good men to the job. With the Vice President working in so much closer intimacy with the President, the conventions would be far less likely to place utter strangers or incipient antagonists on the same ticket. Aspiring presidential and vice-presidential teams could be formed in advance of the conventions to present an already formulated and working partnership. And certainly when a candidate was nominated for the presidency he would exert his influence for the selection of the best available man for the vice-presidential nomination.

New concepts of government are difficult to evolve. The ground must be tested and adjustments made as the actualities appear. It is conceivable that it might take some time before the relationship between the President, the assistant president and the Cabinet could be made smooth, permanent and valuable; but this has been true of all relationships inside the federal government. No one would expect the office of the assistant president to spring into being whole and perfect, the day after inauguration.

Under Thomas E. Dewey and Earl Warren the odds would be strongly in favor of a successful beginning. Thomas E. Dewey and Earl Warren like and respect each other. Both are trained, experienced and proven administrators and hence have not only a common background but a common body of understanding. It would be hard to conceive of any team which could make a better start in creating the assistant presidency or establishing it more firmly within the framework of the federal government.

XIII. In Transit

EARL WARREN is neither genius nor saint. He is a master craftsman in the science of democratic government. Like all active men he has made his quota of mistakes, but they are mistakes of the head and never of the heart. One of his toughest Democratic opponents admits, "You can get Earl Warren in the ring, but at the end of fifteen rounds he comes out with his hair unmussed."

He has expressed himself forthrightly on all the important national and international issues of the day. His press conferences in New York and Philadelphia prior to the 1948 Republican convention were a source of delight to the reporters and columnists, who emphasized his dogged frankness, honesty and willingness to go on the record.

In international politics he has been a consistent advocate of world cooperation. Because of his vantage spot on the Pacific Coast he has become an authority on problems of trade with the Orient. He backs a strong America in a strong United Nations, and he maintains that if this United Nations will not work, we will have to go out and get ourselves one that will. He has enthusiastically supported the Marshall Plan for European recovery, not as a program of relief but as a method of helping those friendly nations who are straining to rebuild their economies and become self-sufficient. He has no wish to interfere with other peoples' forms of government, but he does not think we should give aid to any country which will not work with a United Nations. He believes that the single greatest danger in the world today is military aggression; he is equally determined that we as a nation shall not commit acts of aggression, and that, by the same token, we should keep ourselves so strong and prepared that no other nation would dare risk an act of aggression against us.

Warren has been emphatic in reminding the Republican party that it must once again represent the whole American people, and enunciate a broad program to embrace social security, public health, prepaid medical insurance, housing, education and effective measures to prevent runaway inflation. He is determined that the full resources of our nation shall be utilized to prevent any future depressions, and has called for long-range planning to keep us out of economic difficulty.

His record of accomplishment has been nonpartisan and has cut into every segment of American life. Production has always thrived under his administration, and labor has made important strides forward. In the national economy Warren would work, as he has so successfully worked all his life:

For peaceful labor-management relations through fair collective bargaining.

For the appointment to public office of the ablest men in the country.

For keeping governmental responsibility close to the people.

For the widest possible use of the government to protect all its citizens without overburdening the economy with a topheavy federal structure.

For the reduction of taxes and the amortization of the national debt.

For agricultural research.

For the development and conservation of the country's natural resources.

For the extension of recreational facilities and child welfare.

For the right of every American family to achieve a decent, healthful, reasonably secure life.

Earl Warren has demonstrated the all-important capacity for growth in public service at levels of increasingly greater responsibility. He is still ambitious to tackle big and difficult jobs when he thinks they need doing. He has a sane, progressive approach to economic and social problems. He works quietly, achieves teamwork, deals in terms of understatement, never grows frightened or hysterical. Today he is just coming to the peak of his experience and mental power. As a man of large family without independent means, he knows from experience the problems of most of the American people. He has lived an impeccable public and private life; he hates corruption, waste and bureaucracy in government; any administration in which he shared would be rigorously honest, scientifically organized and amiably run. Above all, he has a deep social conscience, for he does not believe that he is his brother's keeper but rather his brother's friend.

Index